FLUENT IN AI

TEACHING PROMPT ENGINEERING AND THE HUMAN-AI PARTNERSHIP

AARON S. LANGENAUER

CONTENTS

INTRODUCTION

About this book

Dear Reader,

This book isn't just *about* artificial intelligence—it gets inside the human-AI partnership to demonstrate how to *use* AI and how to *teach* students to use it.

To be fair, I'm making some assumptions about you. I assume you already recognize that AI is a force to be reckoned with. I assume you already know a little about AI and don't need another treatise about how it can be ethically used to augment, rather than replace, human intelligence.

I assume you're here because you've been thinking about whether and how to teach students to appropriately, responsibly, and effectively use AI for increased achievement—but you hardly know where to begin, because you yourself have only dipped your toes in the water of AI.

This book is for you.

Central to this book is the idea of being fluent in AI—being able to effortlessly and instinctively leverage the power of AI to increase speed, scale, and quality. You've likely come across the notion that humans won't be replaced by AI, but will instead be replaced by other humans who use it. Being fluent in AI means being in the latter category.

This book will take a tour through AI's landscape and applications. We'll begin with a concise overview of AI's history, contextualizing today's advancements within the technology's broader development. This foundation will lead us to a focused examination of large language models (LLMs) and AI chatbots, which will give us a frame of understanding for exploring the idea of AI fluency. From there, we'll dig into the art and science of prompt engineering—the practice of crafting instructions that elicit high-quality outputs from AI. You'll learn strategies ranging from fundamental concepts to advanced techniques, enabling you to effectively enlist AI's assistance in a diverse array of personal and professional tasks.

After this study of prompt engineering, we'll explore ideas for designing curricula and learning experiences. First, we'll imagine a hypothetical class dedicated to prompt engineering and using AI, digging into the learning goals, performance tasks, and example project-based learning plans.

Then, we'll discuss AI in the larger context of K-12 education and explore a seven-step playbook for integrating AI into the already established education landscape. This will include issues pertaining to professional development, curricular considerations, actionable frameworks, and community transparency.

My hope is that you walk away from this book with knowledge and confidence. You'll understand what AI is (and isn't) capable of, you'll be prepared to apply the technology to make yourself better at any number of different tasks, and you'll have a new perspective on how to make sense of AI in the world of education. In essence, you'll be equipped to develop fluency in AI and be better prepared to teach students to do the same.

I hope this book makes a difference.

Thank you,

Aaron

How I learned about and use AI

I have been a music teacher for 11 years, but I have a long-running fascination with how emerging technologies intersect with the timeless principles of teaching and learning. It's what inspired me to study curriculum development and instructional technology for my graduate work and later earn an advanced certificate in educational leadership, and it was further fueled by my years of experience as an instructional technology coach. So, when I first started to toy around with ChatGPT in the spring of 2023, I—like many others—was immediately struck by its potential.

My "aha!" moment came that April. I was at a conference and was engaging in a discussion with a group of people after a presentation. I don't even remember what the presentation was about, but AI came up in the discussion. I shared that I had been using ChatGPT to rewrite the curriculum (with mixed results) for a class I teach. What struck me was everyone's reaction as I told this story: complete fascination. They had all heard of ChatGPT but hadn't used it, and they were enthralled to hear about my experience. That was when I realized I was onto something, that this was a topic worth really diving into.

I began a journey of intensive self-study. I read some books on the history of artificial intelligence, began following every published news story about AI I could find, and continued my experimentations with various tools. I discovered a community of content creators focused on AI and began following them on social media and signing up for their email newsletters. I read them all religiously. I kept tabs on every trend in AI—technological developments, new tools and features, proposed legislation, copyright lawsuits, and more. I saw how people were using AI to launch entrepreneurial ventures and leave their traditional jobs, showcasing how revolutionary this technology could be for the world my students will inherit.

The more I learned, the more I used AI for both personal and professional tasks. My improving prompt engineering skills allowed me to enlist AI for a wide range of activities:

- Planning meals and grocery lists
- Creating vacation itineraries
- Explaining complicated concepts
- Writing and revising instructional plans
- Developing worksheets and rubrics
- Crafting various written materials, from emails to cover letters to eBooks

I experimented with different tools as they became available—ChatGPT, Claude, Perplexity, Copilot, Bard (later renamed Gemini), and Meta AI. Through this exploration, I learned how each tool's unique features could be leveraged and how subtle changes in prompts could yield significantly different results.

Currently, I use an AI chatbot aggregator platform called Poe. It has free features, but I pay a monthly subscription for it. Through Poe, I can access a variety of different large language models created by different companies. To generate examples of the AI threads in this book, I spread the wealth around what I think of as "The Big Four" chatbots widely accessible to people:

Model	Application	Company
GPT-4o	ChatGPT	OpenAI
Claude-3.5-Sonnet	Claude	Anthropic
Gemini-1.5	Gemini	Google
Llama-3.1	Meta AI	Meta

I often bounce around these models for various tasks, mostly out of curiosity to compare how they perform. AI tools are constantly being updated, so don't put a lot of stock in the next sentence, since things might change by the time you read this book. But as of now (summer 2024), I find GPT-4o to be great for all-around tasks, Claude to be the best writer, and Gemini to be very creative. I cook with GPT-4o, write with Claude, and brainstorm with either those two or Gemini. I admit I haven't used Meta AI enough to make a thorough evaluation of it.

If I want to search the internet for something, I'll use either Gemini (usually through the Google search engine), Copilot (by Microsoft and powered by GPT-4), or Perplexity.ai (which uses multiple models, including ones by OpenAI and Anthropic).

As I gained a reputation for my knowledge about AI, I began giving presentations at various conferences. These talks covered what AI is and isn't, how it's being used across industries in the real world, what it all means for education, and practical tips for how people can start using AI. These experiences provided me with deeper insights into the questions and concerns that teachers and administrators have about AI.

This journey of discovery and experimentation has led me to write this book. I have immersed myself in this world and developed what I think of as fluency in AI. Using AI has become second nature to me. I know what different tools are good at and I know when and how to use them. I can evaluate the responses I get and know how to iterate with an AI to get better results—or when to step back and do things the "old-fashioned" way. By following economic and geopolitical trends, I've come to recognize that humanity has reached an inflection point with this technology, and its impact on education will be extraordinary.

I don't consider myself an AI evangelist. What I am, however, is immensely respectful of this technology (and a bit of a nerd). Just because we *can* use a piece of technology doesn't mean we *should*. But AI is without a doubt a revolutionary force that is turning parts of our world topsy turvy. We need to grapple with it and understand it before we can articulate its role in education.

But there is a vast divide in AI understanding that exists in the education community. My experiences presenting and talking with fellow educators have shown me that while interest in AI is high, practical knowledge is lagging. This realization has become the driving force behind this book. By illuminating what it means to be fluent in AI, I hope to provide a bridge for you and other educators, helping us all to cross the chasm from AI novices to confident practitioners.

How I used AI to write this book

This is the only section of the book untouched by AI (or is it?).

I started this book by drafting an outline of ideas. My plan was to take that outline to an AI and have it provide feedback and suggest additional points to cover. I intended to go back and forth with the AI to develop a comprehensive outline before beginning the actual writing. But halfway through that outline I realized that I already knew what I wanted to say in large portions of this book. So I dug in and began writing.

As I wrote, I regularly turned to AI to help me reword passages and explain ideas in different ways. I would share excerpts with an AI and ask it for suggestions about points to include that I didn't think of. I only took maybe half of those suggestions, but the ones I took were incredibly valuable.

After writing the first draft came the editing. I shared excerpts with AI and had conversations about my writing style. I listed writers I admired and had AI explain to me what made their styles unique and engaging. I spent time—a lot of time—developing prompts where I would share an excerpt of my draft and have the AI rewrite it in the kind of style I was envisioning. Here is an example of such a prompt:

> ***You are an expert editor and writer specializing in best-selling non-fiction books. Your task is to rewrite and**

expand upon the draft book excerpt below. Focus on these key aspects of writing style:

<aspects>

-Maintain clarity and conciseness, expressing complex ideas in straightforward language.

-Adopt an authoritative tone that conveys expertise and confidence.

-Incorporate relevant analogies or metaphors to explain complex concepts.

-If applicable, create an engaging opening that hooks the reader.

-Present a balanced structure, considering multiple perspectives before offering analysis.

-Inject subtle humor or wit.

-Use succinct paragraphs to aid readability and maintain attention.

</aspects>

Additionally, your key objectives are to:

<objectives>

-Identify and expand upon the main ideas in the original text.

-Provide supporting details, examples, or context to enhance reader understanding.

-Ensure that each point is fully developed and clearly explained.

-Add relevant information or insights that complement the original ideas.

-Maintain a logical flow between ideas, enhancing over-all coherence.

</objectives>

Remember to preserve the core message from the orig-inal text and maintain its layout and its sections, while transforming its style to match the description above and expand on the content. The draft may include conver-sations with an AI, which will be marked by delimiters. These AI conversations cannot be changed, and your re-written draft should only notate where the AI conversa-tions go via placeholder brackets without actually includ-ing them. Do not rewrite them, but you may write about them and refer to them.

If your rewritten draft is too long for one response, then write as much as is allowed and then let me know that there is more to include. I will then instruct you to contin-ue your draft and we will repeat this process until you let me know that you are finished. Here's the draft to rewrite and expand:

<draft>

[draft excerpt]

</draft>

Don't worry, every aspect of this prompt will make sense af-ter reading Chapter 4.

In the meantime, now is probably a good time to discuss for-matting in this book. Prompts will be formatted like the one above: indented, bold, and beginning with an asterisk. AI re-sponses will be similarly indented but italicized. AI responses have only been edited for formatting purposes.

*Here is an example of a prompt.

Here is an example of an AI response.

Anyway, the detailed prompt above surprisingly gave me mixed results. There were a lot of rewritten excerpts I liked, but too many of them missed the mark. They just didn't sound like *my* writing, even though I was aiming for what I described in the prompt. And to be clear, the AI did a great job following my instructions. But there was clearly a disconnect between what I wanted and what I was describing. Welcome to prompt engineering.

I then tried a different approach that worked much better, using this prompt with Claude-3.5-Sonnet:

> ***I just hired you as my ghostwriter and editor. I am going to share a draft excerpt of my book with you. I want you to summarize the key ideas and provide feedback on the writing:**
>
> **[draft excerpt]**

Summarizing the key ideas was the most important ingredient. It was an intermediate step I added that made the whole task of editing and rewriting longer, but it allowed me some great opportunities (foreshadowing for Chapter 3). If the summarized ideas were not what I intended to communicate in my writing, I went back and forth with the AI to make my ideas clearer and rewrite the outline it provided. I also had it show me examples of how it could implement its suggestions, like drafting a paragraph explaining a point it recommended including. After some back and forth, I would eventually tell the AI to rewrite my original draft to incorporate all the changes we discussed—meaning any revised outlines and its suggestions that I accepted.

This workflow pattern enabled the AI to maintain my original voice but improve the writing.

But the process didn't end there. I would copy and paste the revised AI-generated draft into my document and then begin *ruthlessly* editing. I probably cut at least a third of the words, paragraphs, and passages it wrote. There were times I accepted the revised phrasing of my words and other times when I stuck with the original, and many times when I combined the two. After completing the first draft, I went through the whole book again with a fine-tooth comb and did a lot more editing and rewriting.

The result was a combination of human-generated and AI-generated writing woven together. Keep an eye out for the subtle differences in tone and style. In fact, I offer this challenge: Throughout this book, see if you can distinguish between the two. It won't be as easy as you think. (Here's a hint: AI wrote one sentence in this paragraph.)

And after all of that, I still worked with a human editor. Why? After all, AI was a significant help in allowing me to more fully develop ideas, explore different ways of explaining things, and catch details I would have missed. The result was certainly a book that's "well-written" by any conventional measure. But it was still a book that *I* wrote in *my* writing style. The problem is that this book isn't for me—it's for you. Just because my writing style and explanations make sense to me doesn't mean they'll make sense for you, and I needed an editor to act as your lawyer and go through the book arguing in defense of how *you'll* experience it.

AI could help me to execute the tasks that built this book, but it couldn't help me ensure that this book is the solution I originally envisioned. To do that, I needed real expertise.

I needed a human.

CHAPTER
01

HOW WE GOT HERE

Let's begin with a high-level look at how artificial intelligence research has evolved to get to today's state of play. This overview isn't meant to be exhaustive or highly detailed. Instead, it aims to offer essential context for understanding how AI works and how it has become the transformative force we see today.

By understanding this evolution, we'll be better equipped to assess both the capabilities and limitations of current AI technologies. Why is this broader perspective so important? Because AI is a technology that cannot be effectively *used* until it's comprehensively *understood.*

A brief history of AI, part 1

A history of artificial intelligence could start at any number of points (Greek mythology, the first computers, the Turing test, etc.). But for our purposes, let's begin with the first iteration of the term "artificial intelligence," in 1956 at a summer camp for scientists.

At that time, a group of scientists convened at Dartmouth College for the Dartmouth Summer Research Project on Artificial Intelligence (and hence the infamous term). The purpose of this conference was to explore the idea that aspects of learning and intelligence could be precisely described and then simulated by a machine. Read that last sentence again because it's important. This moment is considered the birth of artificial intelligence as a field of study.

Coming out of this event, the 1950s and 1960s saw significant enthusiasm for this new field of research. This enthusiasm was fueled by new AI endeavors across academic institutions, the rapid advancement of computing power, and some notable successes, such as:

- The Logic Theorist, a program able to successfully prove mathematical theorems

- The development of the perceptron, which simulated the functioning of a human neuron and laid the foundation for neural networks
- ELIZA, an early chatbot that simulated conversations with a psychotherapist
- The development of Natural Language Processing, with researchers creating programs capable of understanding simple sentences and responding in a rudimentary manner

Many bold claims were made during this time about how computers would soon rival humans in intelligence (spoiler alert: they didn't). But a combination of critical reports and unmet expectations then led to what is now known as the AI Winter. During this time in the 1970s and 1980s, a lot of the funding that fueled the research of the prior decades dried up, and artificial intelligence receded into the background of the scientific community.

Despite the chill of the AI Winter, research persisted, even if it wasn't front-page news. The idealism of simulating human-like intelligence gave way to more practical applications throughout the 1970s and 1980s. Researchers turned their attention to developing programs that could emulate expertise in narrow domains to accomplish specialized tasks. These were called expert systems.

A famous example is MYCIN, a program able to diagnose and prescribe treatment for bacterial blood infections at a level comparable to human specialists. It accomplished this by using a series of pre-written rules about the medical domain and logical "if this, then that" programming to interpret reported symptoms and lab results.

Expert systems proved useful, but their limitations became clear. To better understand why and what happened next, we need to pause and focus on three key ideas that are crucial for understanding the development and current state of AI.

Side notes: AGI, symbolic AI, and machine learning

The first key idea is the distinction between Artificial General Intelligence (AGI) and Narrow Artificial Intelligence. AGI is what scientists were initially aiming for at the Dartmouth conference in 1956—the ability for computers to simulate all of human knowledge and learning. This is science fiction AI: computers and robots able to rival, or even exceed, human levels of accomplishment in advanced cognitive tasks.

Perspectives on AGI range widely. At one extreme, advocates see it as the opportunity for a utopia where all our needs are met by machines far more capable than we are. At the other, critics view AGI as a threat that could lead to the destruction of humankind. It's a story of "boomers" vs. "doomers." Most people fall somewhere in between, optimistic about AI's potential to solve major problems like renewable energy and disease, but concerned about issues such as misinformation and data privacy.

AGI does not currently exist, but it's important to be aware of because much of today's AI developments are driven by the quest for this holy grail. In contrast, all of today's AI programs fall under Narrow AI, which focuses on leveraging AI to solve specific problems or complete specific tasks. This includes everything from expert systems like MYCIN to all of the AI tools at our disposal today. Even ChatGPT is still considered Narrow AI, since its abilities are limited to text generation.[1] But it's worth noting that the company behind it, OpenAI, is public about its goals for developing AGI.

The second key idea is about how AI programs functioned from the 1950s to the 1980s. This era was dominated by symbolic AI, where pieces of information are encoded as symbols to be manipulated by the AI program. These programs are essentially governed by a combination of knowledge and rules—

---

1 ChatGPT can be used to generate images, but it uses a separate image-generation model, called DALL-E, to do so.

MYCIN being a prime example. Despite some successes, symbolic AI had severe limitations. These systems struggled to account for anomalies, their "knowledge" was difficult to update, they were resource-intensive to maintain, and they could only accomplish very specific tasks. In essence, they weren't well-suited for the messiness of the real world.

Expert systems like MYCIN therefore showcased the potential use cases for AI, but a new approach would be necessary to make AI's use in the real world viable.

This brings us to our third key idea: machine learning, which came to the forefront in the 1990s. Rather than rely on preprogrammed rules and knowledge, machine learning programs analyze massive amounts of data to discover patterns and relationships, forming their own understanding of the world.

To illustrate the difference, consider a self-driving car that needs to recognize bicycles. With symbolic AI, engineers would need to create an exhaustive list of rules about what bicycles look like—every color, shape, size, accessory, etc., and every combination thereof. But with machine learning, the engineers could simply provide the AI with millions of pictures of bicycles, allowing it to determine on its own how to recognize them.

Machine learning encompasses various approaches. The bicycle example showcases supervised learning, which uses labeled data (ex. [picture] = bicycle). Unsupervised learning discovers patterns in unlabeled data (ex. discovering patterns in consumer data), and semi-supervised learning combines elements of both.

While the theoretical foundations of machine learning were laid in the earliest days of AI research, it required two things that weren't available until the late 20th century: powerful computers and massive amounts of data.

A brief history of AI, part 2

This brings us back to our AI timeline. As computers became ubiquitous in homes and businesses, and as the world increasingly connected through the internet, vast amounts of data became accessible to researchers. This coincided with advances in computing power, making the practical application of machine learning theories possible on a large scale in the 1990s and 2000s.

One of the big ideas that gained traction during this period was the neural network, a cornerstone of modern machine learning. Work on this concept actually started in the 1950s, inspired by the human brain's structure and function. In a neural network, software units called perceptrons mimic the role of neurons in the brain. Just as activity in one neuron can trigger activity in connected neurons, perceptrons in a network influence each other based on the strength of their connections.

Neural networks proved exceptionally adept at "learning" through exposure to numerous examples. If an AI program knows the correct answer to something (like identifying a bicycle in an image), it can compare that correct answer to the output generated by its neural network. If the output is incorrect, the program adjusts the weights governing the relationships between its perceptrons and repeats this process until it consistently generates the correct answer. This error correction and learning process is called backpropagation.

As machine learning, powered by neural networks, took the lead in AI research, the world witnessed notable achievements in AI. These included advancements in speech and language recognition programs and the early development of self-driving cars.

This trend accelerated dramatically in the 2000s and 2010s. The proliferation of internet-connected devices and the rise of social media led to an unprecedented explosion in available data. Researchers also discovered that graphics processing units (GPUs), originally designed for gaming computers, were highly effective at running neural networks. This led to the development of deep learning—the use of neural networks with many layers of perceptrons, allowing for more complex pattern recognition and decision-making.

As a result of these developments, AI began to permeate many aspects of daily life. Recommendation systems on platforms like Amazon and Netflix, personalized social media feeds, targeted political campaigns, voice assistants on smartphones and smart devices, and functional self-driving cars all emerged during this period, showcasing the practical applications of advanced machine learning techniques. The world entered the era of big data.

Then, in 2017, a breakthrough called the transformer model revolutionized natural language processing. Before this innovation, AI programs could only process text sequentially, one word at a time. The transformer model allowed AI to analyze larger units of text, such as sentences or paragraphs, simultaneously. This dramatically improved AI's ability to understand the relationships between words and process vast amounts of text at unprecedented speeds.

The transformer model's impact on natural language processing set the stage for a new era in AI development. In 2022, OpenAI released ChatGPT, a large language model with an ability to engage in human-like conversations, answer complex questions, and generate coherent text across a wide range of topics and styles (a similar program wrote the first draft of this paragraph). Built on the foundation of the transformer architecture, ChatGPT represented a quantum leap in AI capabilities, demonstrating an unprecedented level of language understanding and generation.

The launch of ChatGPT will likely be remembered as marking the beginning of the current age of generative AI, where machines can not only process and analyze information but also create new content—be it text, images, or even code—that is often indistinguishable from human-created work. This breakthrough has sparked a new wave of AI applications and services, revolutionizing industries from healthcare to customer service to content creation and software development.

It now seems like AI is touching every part of our lives. There are new stories every day. Some are positive (like how AI is being used to solve problems in healthcare, sustainable energy, and agriculture), and some are negative (like how AI is being used to create disinformation or replace human jobs). The debate between boomers and doomers rages on, but one thing is clear: we've arrived at the future.

Artificial intelligence is not a "thing"

One common misconception in discussions about artificial intelligence is evident in the way people often phrase questions or statements about its use. When people ask, "How can we use AI?", it suggests a view of AI as a singular, monolithic tool rather than a diverse field of technologies and approaches.

This phrasing oversimplifies the complex nature of AI and can lead to ineffective or misguided implementation strategies. It's akin to asking, "How can we use science?" —the question is so broad that it becomes almost meaningless without further context or specificity.

A more informed approach would involve asking about specific AI technologies or applications that might address particular needs or challenges. In education, for example, we might ask:

- "How can we use natural language processing to improve writing feedback?"
- "Could machine learning algorithms help us identify students at risk of falling behind?"

- "In what ways could AI-powered adaptive learning platforms personalize instruction?"

By framing questions and discussions in this more specific manner, stakeholders and decision-makers demonstrate a clearer understanding of AI's diverse nature and are more likely to identify and implement effective AI-driven solutions.

It is, however, perfectly appropriate to refer to an individual tool as "an AI" or "the AI" (and I will continue to do so in this book). We just have to remember that artificial intelligence is an entire field of study, not a single technology.

AI is a subset of computer science that itself encompasses various approaches, such as symbolic AI and machine learning. These different approaches have yielded a diverse array of innovations and applications.

An apt comparison is to think of the term "artificial intelligence" like the term "classical music." While we often use "classical music" as a catch-all term, it actually encompasses multiple distinct periods, styles, and types of compositions. Just as a Haydn string quartet and a Mahler symphony are two very different types of musical works (despite both being labeled as "classical"), an LLM chatbot, a self-driving car, and an industry-specific data analysis tool are all very different technologies resulting from different approaches to artificial intelligence.

So, while it's perfectly fine to talk about specific AI tools or applications in narrow terms, it's important to remember that AI isn't really a singular "thing", but a rich and diverse field of study. This understanding is crucial as we navigate discussions about AI's impact, potential, and future development. By recognizing the breadth and diversity of AI, we can have more nuanced and productive conversations about its role in education.

Why the skeptics are right

While I assume that, by reading this book, you've embraced (or are at least curious about) the promises and potential of AI, it's worth pointing out that skeptics have legitimate concerns regarding unfounded hype and overinflated expectations. Many teachers and administrators are rightfully cautious about adopting technologies that promise to revolutionize teaching and learning, only to fall short of these lofty claims.

The research firm Gartner developed a model for under-standing trends in emerging technologies that helps illustrate this point. The Gartner Hype Cycle describes five phases in a new technology's life, and we can clearly see the history of AI following this cycle:

- **Phase 1: The Innovation Trigger**. A breakthrough, product release, or media interest sparks enthusiasm and publicity.
  - **AI example**: The Dartmouth Summer Research Project in 1956

- **Phase 2: The Peak of Inflated Expectations**. Early successes lead to bold claims about how the new technology will be revolutionary.
  - **AI example**: The research funding, achievements, and excitement of the 1950s-1960s

- **Phase 3: The Trough of Disillusionment**. Interest declines after the technology underdelivers on evangelists' bold claims.
  - **AI example**: The AI Winter of the 1970s

- **Phase 4: The Slope of Enlightenment**. The realistic applications of the technology that survived the burst bubble begin to crystallize, and more targeted applications start to emerge.
  - **AI example**: Expert systems in the 1980s and machine learning in the 1990s

- **Phase 5: The Plateau of Productivity**. Mainstream adoption takes shape as the applications of the technology are verified.

  - **AI example**: Big data and deep learning in the 2000s-2010s

Below is my sloppy and unartistic visual representation of this cycle:

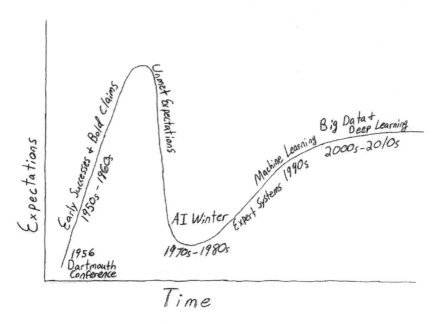

It's worth pointing out an important caveat: Gartner says a technology typically takes 3-5 years to make its way through the hype cycle, whereas I've illustrated a 50+ year cycle. One could also argue that machine learning is its own innovation separate from the symbolic AI approach of earlier decades and therefore warrants the start of a new cycle. Nevertheless, I still think the relationship between the Gartner Hype Cycle and history of AI makes a compelling case for looking at AI through both its short-term and long-term expectations.

It's also reasonable to claim that the release of ChatGPT in 2022 sparked a new cycle for generative AI, and this is where skeptics in education have a valid point. The education space is filled with promises about how AI will revolutionize teaching and learning, but we must admit that we could be in the inflated expectations phase of this technology. It's quite possible this enthusiasm will fade away in a few years after a period of overpromising and underdelivering, leaving educators disillusioned and hesitant to adopt future AI technologies.

Even so, I want to contrast the prevalence and abilities of AI in the 1960s with that in the 2010s. Even if the innovations and claims of early AI evangelists failed to yield machines that could rival human cognition, we nonetheless ended up with voice assistants and self-driving cars a half-century later.

And this is the point I want to emphasize now: even if current claims about generative AI are overinflated, we should still plan for the world that will take shape further in the future.

In fact, we *should* be skeptical of bold claims made by companies, consultants, and publications (present company included) about how a given technology or product will change everything in education in the near future. But we also need to think about and plan for how the educational landscape will look when realistic applications of generative AI impact the ways people learn, teach, and create. Followers of technology and business news know that this has already started to happen.

Hence, the importance of understanding and interacting with AI becomes paramount. No matter how AI's role in education evolves in the coming years, the ability to partner and interact with AI in the real world will be a core skill across all professions—and success in using AI will boil down to the ability to effectively communicate with these systems and critically evaluate their output.

This is why it's important to understand the underlying technology behind generative AI. In the next chapter, we'll delve into large language models, the systems behind tools like ChatGPT. By understanding how these models work, their capabilities, and their limitations, we can better navigate the hype cycle and make informed decisions about integrating AI into educational practices.

But more importantly, this understanding will prepare us for why you're really here: mastering, and then teaching, prompt engineering.

CHAPTER
02

UNDERSTANDING LARGE LANGUAGE MODELS

Generative artificial intelligence refers to AI systems that can create various types of content—text, image, audio, video, and code that is not part of the AI's training data. For the purposes of this book, I'm going to focus specifically on text-based large language models (LLMs). There are two main reasons for this approach.

First, I wrote this book with a realistic view of what students and teachers will likely be able to access in the coming years. There's a massive divide between AI tools available in the real world and those accessible in the classroom (more on that in Chapter 6). While AI-powered educational tools are entering the market, most of these tools currently revolve around text-based LLM chatbots. In an effort to focus on the core concepts and skills with the widest applicability, independent of specific tools, LLMs will be our focus.

The second reason is that fluency in AI is a transferrable skill. By mastering AI interaction in the context of LLMs, you'll develop a foundation that can later be applied to generating images and other forms of content. Becoming fluent in AI leads to the confidence and know-how to explore and master any new kind of AI tool.

So, while this book is limited to LLMs and text-based generative AI, keep in mind that the mindset you'll develop and the skills you'll acquire here will lay the groundwork for understanding and commanding all sorts of AI technologies in the future. This approach ensures that the skills you learn will remain relevant and applicable, even as AI technology continues to evolve rapidly in both educational and real-world contexts.

What LLMs are trained to do

Large language models are built on a foundation of mind-boggling amounts of data. To put it in perspective, if a human tried to read every piece of text that GPT-3.5 (the model behind ChatGPT when it was released in 2022) was trained on, it would take thousands of lifetimes of non-stop reading, 24 hours a day. And newer LLMs have been trained on even more data. But here's the kicker—these models don't learn facts like we do. Instead, they learn patterns and relationships between words.

For instance, an LLM will observe that the word "dog" often appears near words like "bark", "tail", and "walk". The LLM takes these words (represented as tokens, which we'll get into later) and turns them into numbers called word vectors. Think of these vectors as points in a multidimensional space—kind of like a super complex version of latitude and longitude.

Let's look at an example. In our world, latitude and longitude coordinates show that New York City and Philadelphia are close to each other, and London and Paris are close to each other, but the first pair is far away from the second pair. In the LLM's world of word vectors, "cat" and "dog" might be close to each other, "violin" and "cello" might be close to each other, but these two pairs would be far apart (unless we're talking about a very avant-garde orchestra).

So, how does an LLM use all this to generate responses? Let's say we ask a chatbot, "Who was president of the United States in 1955?" It's almost certain to respond with "Dwight Eisenhower." But here's the thing—it's not because the chatbot *knows* this as a fact in the way we do. Instead, when it processes the words "president", "United States", and "1955", it performs complex mathematical calculations to determine the most probable continuation of words based on the patterns it has learned. In this case, it concludes that "Dwight Eisenhower" is the most likely correct answer, as opposed to Harry Truman or John Kennedy.

Model vs. Application

Let's take a moment now to clear up a common source of confusion: the difference between an LLM and the application that uses it. Think of the LLM as an engine, and the application as the car it powers.

For example, GPT-4 is the engine—the underlying language model trained on vast amounts of data. It's the powerhouse that processes text and generates responses. ChatGPT, on the other hand, is the sleek sports car built around that engine. It's the user-friendly interface that lets you interact with GPT-4.

This distinction matters for a few reasons:

1. **Capabilities and Limitations**: The raw model might be capable of tasks that the application doesn't expose to users, and some limitations you experience might be due to the application, not the underlying model. It's like having an engine capable of going 200 mph but limiting the car to 120 mph for safety reasons. Maybe a given chatbot can't search the internet, but that's not because the model can't understand web pages—it's a design choice for the application.

2. **Updates**: The application and the underlying models could be updated at different times, like how Google will update Android, but Samsung has its own process and timeline for updating its Android-powered Galaxy phones. This is important to know when using an application built on top of another company's LLM.

3. **Specialization**: Different applications can use the same model for varied purposes. GPT-4 powers ChatGPT, but it's also the brain behind Microsoft's Copilot. Same engine, different vehicles—and different application features.

Understanding this distinction helps explain why you might hear about capabilities of GPT-4 that you can't access through an AI application powered by it, or why different AI tools powered by the same model might behave differently. It's all about how the application is designed to harness and channel the raw power of the underlying LLM.

Now, with that distinction clear, let's talk about how you can steer these AI-powered vehicles with the right prompts. The prompt you give an LLM guides it in interpreting its understanding of word relationships and influences how it calculates what word should come next. We'll explore later on (in *great* detail) how prompt engineering strategies influence an LLM's output. For now, suffice it to say that prompt engineering is like the steering wheel—the engine could be incredibly powerful, and the car could have tons of features, but only the driver tells it where to go (apocalyptic visions of self-driving cars aside).

Some technical extras

Now, let's dive into some of the more technical aspects that work behind the scenes in LLMs: tokens, context windows, and parameters. Boring? Yes. Important to know? Also yes.

When we talk about LLMs, "tokens" are the basic units of text that the model processes. They can be whole words, parts of words, or even individual characters, depending on the specific tokenization method used.

For example, the word "hamburger" might be split into tokens like "ham", "bur", and "ger". On the other hand, a common word like "the" would likely be a single token. This tokenization process is crucial because it's how the LLM breaks down and understands text.

Tokens also play a big role in the "context window". Think of the context window as the LLM's short-term memory. It's the amount of text (measured in tokens) that the model can consider at any given time when generating a response. Different LLMs have different context windows. If you were to upload an entire novel into an LLM, it would likely be unable to process all that data in one prompt because the novel would exceed its context window.

Likewise, you might notice the LLM's behavior change over the course of a *very* long thread for the same reason (like getting to the end of a season of that show you like and then your partner turns to you and asks, "wait, who's that guy again?"). A larger context window allows the LLM to maintain coherence over longer conversations or documents, and to draw connections between ideas that are farther apart in the text.

Additionally, there are several the behind-the-scenes parameters that influence how an LLM responds. One of the most important is called "temperature" (which has nothing to do with your computer overheating).

Temperature refers to how "creative" or "random" the model's outputs are. A lower temperature makes the model more deterministic and focused, always choosing the most probable next word. This is great for tasks where you want consistent, predictable responses. On the other hand, a higher temperature introduces more randomness. The model might choose words with lower probability, leading to more diverse and potentially more creative outputs. This can be useful for brainstorming or creative tasks, but it also increases the chance of the model saying something unexpected or even nonsensical.

Temperature is only one example. There are other parameters too, but here's the key point: as a typical user chatting with an AI, you don't get to fiddle with these knobs directly. They're usually pre-set to balanced values that work well for general conversation and customized for that specific application.

So, who does get to play with these settings? It varies:

1. The folks who created the LLM set some parameters during the model's training. These are baked into the model and aren't typically changed after the fact.

2. Developers using the LLM's Application Programming Interface (API) are often able to adjust parameters like temperature. They use this to fine-tune the AI's behavior for specific tasks or applications. These folks are essentially taking the model/engine, making some tweaks, and customizing it for the car they're designing.

3. Some consumer-facing AI tools or specialized chatbots might give you, the end user, control over a simplified version of these settings. You might see a "creativity" slider, for instance, which adjusts the temperature behind the scenes.

But for your average user having a chat with an AI assistant? These parameters are like the gears in a watch—essential for making everything tick, but not something you typically fiddle with.

So, why is this important to know? Because understanding that these parameters exist, even if we can't always control them, helps explain the differences in behavior among LLMs, why the same AI might give slightly different responses to the same question, or why it might seem more creative in some contexts than others.

This understanding can also help us to evaluate AI applications and tools. For example, a vendor might advertise that its educational AI chatbot has minimal risks of hallucination—but that might be because they set the temperature way down, which also reduces the chatbot's creativity.

To wrap this all up, let's consider how all these elements work together. When you input a prompt, the LLM tokenizes it and processes it within its context window. It then uses its vast network of word relationships, fine-tuned by parameters like temperature, to calculate the most probable (or appropriately random) next tokens. This process repeats for each word in the response, creating a coherent output that can range from factual and focused to creative and diverse, depending on how it's configured (and how the user prompted the AI in the first place).

Understanding these concepts—from tokenization to context windows to adjustable parameters—gives us insight into both the capabilities and limitations of LLMs. It helps explain why they can produce responses that are inconsistent or unreliable, but also responses that are incredibly knowledgeable, surprisingly insightful, and wonderfully creative.

Internet access can be bittersweet

LLMs are trained on vast amounts of data up to a specific point in time. When ChatGPT was released in 2022, for example, its training data only went up to 2021. This cutoff date is often misunderstood as a limitation, with some people assuming it means the LLM doesn't have current information. But because you've read this far, you now know better.

Recall that LLMs are designed to generate responses based on patterns and relationships in their training data, rather than to provide real-time information. Just like LLMs don't "know" facts, they also don't actively search a database of information to inform their responses (with a caveat we'll visit when we look at advanced prompt engineering). So, the end-point of their training data is actually irrelevant for the tasks they excel at.

But AI could still be helpful for finding and summarizing up-to-date information—you just need to use a different tool. For these tasks, there are AI-powered "answer engines" that can search the internet and summarize the responses while citing their sources. Examples include Perplexity, Microsoft's Copilot, and Google's AI Overview search feature. These tools bridge the gap between traditional LLMs and current data needs.

But internet access is not always a good thing.

Understanding the task at hand is key to deciding which AI tool is most appropriate. When tackling creative tasks or brainstorming ideas, I prefer using an LLM without internet access. For instance, if I'm using an AI tool to write a unit plan, I don't want it limiting its possible responses to instructional plans others have already created and posted online. Instead, I want something more creative and customized to my unique needs.

To accomplish that goal, I want to leverage the LLM's understanding of language patterns (and my well-written prompts that directed it) to create something new and original, while relying on my own expertise to evaluate its output.

On the other hand, AI-complemented internet searching can be game-changing for other tasks. Whether exploring flights to book, researching product features, or summarizing recent developments in a topic, chatbots with internet access can offer significant benefits. These tools can quickly gather, compare, and synthesize information from multiple sources, saving time and providing comprehensive overviews.

Ultimately, effective use of AI tools comes down to understanding what you're trying to accomplish and how different tools function. By recognizing the strengths of both internet-connected and non-connected AI tools, you can choose the most appropriate tool for the task at hand.

Why LLMs are bad at math

Large language models calculate words, not numbers. To an AI, two plus two equals four not because it's performing the addition, but because it's calculating that the *words* "two plus two equals..." are most likely followed by the *word* "four."

Chain-of-Thought prompting, which we'll discuss in Chapter 4, has been a popular strategy to work around this limitation. This technique encourages the AI to break down complex problems into smaller, manageable steps. LLMs are becoming increasingly adept at doing this automatically, even without explicit prompting.[2] However, the accuracy of these breakdowns can still vary across different models and problem types.

For example, when I tested various models with a problem about calculating real investment returns after inflation, most

---

2   In September of 2024, OpenAI released previews of its GPT-o1 model, which automatically utilizes an advanced chain-of-thought technique.

broke down the problem into steps without prompting. Yet, the responses differed between models, and some still made errors in their calculations.

As these models continue to evolve, it's likely that AI mathematical capabilities will improve. We might soon see LLMs integrated with specialized calculators, a development that would likely coincide with advancements in "agents"—AI programs capable of determining and executing sequential steps to complete complex tasks without explicit instructions for each subtask (and possibly the precursor to killer robots). In this scenario, an LLM would recognize that math needs to be calculated and would then hand things over to its connected calculator software; the calculator would then hand the solution back over to the LLM to continue with its original task.

Given these current limitations and the rapid pace of development in AI math capabilities, this book will focus primarily on language tasks. This focus is not only practical given the current state of LLMs but also strategic. As discussed previously, AI fluency is highly transferable. Whether you're using AI for writing, analysis, or even future mathematical applications, the fluency you gain in AI interaction will serve you well across all domains.

Hallucinations (and why we should like them)

Because LLMs are trained on the relationships between words, their responses are based on language patterns and probabilities, not facts. This means that an AI's response might include inaccurate information, known as a hallucination.

Hallucinations are often referenced when criticizing AI. The argument goes that, because AI's factual accuracy isn't a guarantee, it's dangerous to rely on AI.

However, I would argue that the problem isn't the technology, but how the technology is used. Without an understanding of how LLMs work, there is indeed a risk of relying on something unreliable, just as there's a risk of inadvertently relying on inaccurate information gleaned from the internet. But with the knowledge of how LLMs construct their responses, hallucinations become a feature, not a bug.

Earlier, we explored why an LLM could be reasonably expected to correctly name Dwight Eisenhower as the president of the United States in 1955. But what if we threw at it a hypothetical scenario that required thinking out of the box? Here's that thread with Claude-3.5-Sonnet:

*Who was president of the United States in the 1950s in a world in which World War 2 was interrupted by an alien invasion?

This is an intriguing alternate history scenario! In a world where World War 2 was interrupted by an alien invasion, the trajectory of global politics and leadership would likely be dramatically different from our actual history.

Given the radical departure from real events, it's difficult to predict with any certainty who might have become president of the United States in the 1950s under those circumstances. The alien invasion would have fundamentally reshaped geopolitics, alliances, and likely the entire structure of government and society.

Some possibilities to consider:

- *A military leader who played a key role in combating the alien threat might have risen to prominence and been elected president.*

- *The crisis could have led to the suspension of normal democratic processes, potentially resulting in an extended term for the president who was in office at the time of the invasion (Franklin D. Roosevelt, if the timeline diverged in the early 1940s).*

- *The alien invasion might have prompted international cooperation on an unprecedented scale, potentially leading to a more globally-oriented leadership structure rather than traditional nation-state presidencies.*

- *Depending on the outcome of the alien invasion, the very concept of the United States as we know it might not exist in the 1950s of this alternate timeline.*

Without more details about the nature and outcome of the alien invasion, it's impossible to make a definitive statement about who would be president in this scenario. Would you like to explore any particular aspects of this alternate history further?

*Determine who would have been president in the 1950s in this scenario without any additional information.

I understand you want me to determine a specific president for this scenario without additional context. However, I want to emphasize that any answer I provide would be purely speculative and not based on factual information.

Given the constraints, I'll create a plausible fictional scenario:

In this alternate history, let's say the alien invasion occurred in 1943, disrupting World War II. The nations of Earth united to repel the invaders, with the conflict lasting until 1947. In the aftermath, a hero of the alien war was elected as U.S. President:

President James "Skyfall" Anderson (1949-1957)

Anderson was a former Air Force pilot who played a crucial role in the final battle against the alien forces. His leadership during the crisis and his message of rebuilding and unity resonated with the American people, leading to his election in 1948 and re-election in 1952.

This is, of course, entirely fictional. In questions like this about extremely speculative alternate histories, I may inadvertently generate details that could be considered hallucinations. The name, backstory, and even the concept of a war hero becoming president are all inventions based on the scenario you provided.

This exchange illustrates two crucial points about AI and hallucinations:

1. **Responsible AI use**: I must admit I was surprised by the initial response. Notice how the AI warned against relying on it for factual information in this speculative scenario. It listed multiple possibilities, emphasized the uncertainty involved, and later highlighted its own potential hallucinations. This kind of transparent communication about its limitations is a key feature of well-designed AI systems, and it's an important consideration in the debate over AI reliability. (This may also be part of why Common Sense Media—at the time of writing—labels Claude as having "minimal" risk.)

2. **Creative potential**: When pressed to provide a specific answer, the AI introduced a fictional character—James "Skyfall" Anderson. This highlights the AI's creative capabilities. A human, constrained by knowledge of historical facts, might struggle to identify a plausible historical figure not known in history textbooks. We might instead follow a line of logic like, "Well, Roosevelt might do this... and Stalin might do that... therefore..." Because AI isn't similarly handcuffed, it can help us overcome the limitations of our own knowledge and spark creative thinking.

While the AI's response was indeed a hallucination, it still showcased an important advantage of AI reasoning: the ability to introduce novel elements not bound by our existing factual knowledge. This untethering from established facts is what allows for incredibly creative responses, whether we're crafting lesson plans, devising vacation itineraries, or exploring speculative scenarios.

It's worth noting that even in hallucinations, there is still factual knowledge at play. The close association between words that form an AI's response is based on a vast database of information. For this reason, I have personally found AI to be very helpful in learning about complex topics and ideas. Even if an AI's response requires fact-checking, its ability to construct a response tailored to my questions and needs has proven to be an incredible learning tool.

Here's the key takeaway about hallucinations: Every AI-generated response is a hallucination, because every response is a novel combination of words yielded from the AI's understanding of written language. Hallucinations are therefore an incredible advantage to be embraced in the pursuit of complex tasks—when we view them as an opportunity for creative output.

That's what being fluent in AI is all about. Shall we unpack that a little more?

CHAPTER
03

BECOMING FLUENT IN AI

Partnership

Now that you know a lot more about what AI is and isn't and how it works, it's time to talk about AI fluency.

What does it mean to be "fluent" in AI? Just as language fluency allows for effortless communication, AI fluency enables the seamless integration of artificial intelligence into your workflow. It's the ability to leverage AI effectively from the moment you conceive an idea to its final execution.

Consider a marketing professional creating a comprehensive campaign for a new product. AI fluency would allow them to:

1. **Recognize AI's potential**: Identify areas where AI could enhance their work, such as data analysis, content generation, or image creation.

2. **Choose the right tool**: Select the most appropriate AI platform for each task, whether it's a language model for copywriting or a web browser add-on for formatting a spreadsheet.

3. **Communicate effectively**: Craft precise instructions (prompts) that elicit high-quality, relevant outputs from the chosen AI tools.

4. **Evaluate critically**: Assess the AI-generated content and determine its relevance, accuracy, and alignment with the campaign goals.

5. **Iterate and refine**: Decide whether to refine the prompts, edit the AI output, or complete certain tasks manually for optimal results.

This scenario illustrates how AI fluency is more than knowing how to use a tool. It's about instinctively blending human creativity and expertise with AI capabilities, resulting in higher-quality work.

Blending the two—human and machine—opens a world of possibilities. Becoming fluent in AI yields significant improvements in the efficiency and quality of work. It will help to generate more creative ideas, plan complex projects, and execute tasks efficiently. The result is the creation of higher-quality outputs, as AI fluency combines the best of human creativity with the technology's analytical and processing powers.

Moreover, AI fluency opens doors to innovation. It allows for rapid prototyping and testing of new ideas and can provide insights that spark novel approaches to challenges old and new. In a competitive landscape, those fluent in AI can punch above their weight, leveraging AI to offer services and solutions typically reserved for much larger teams or those with more resources.

The spoils go to those who take advantage.

You're in charge

It may sound cliché, but the most important part of AI fluency is *the human user's mindset*. It's easy to type something into a chatbot, be unhappy with its output, and claim that the tool doesn't meet the hype (or the opposite—copying and pasting the output without any critical evaluation). But the problem isn't just poor prompt writing or lack of oversight. The original sin is not being clear about what was supposed to be accomplished in the first place.

This brings us to the core concept of AI fluency: the primacy of human direction. When using AI, you're not just a user; you're the director, the decision-maker, the superhero with an AI sidekick. You're enlisting the assistance of a capable but junior partner. In this human-AI partnership, you're the one who sets the direction, evaluates progress, and makes the final calls. The buck stops with you.

Easier said than done.

To effectively partner with an AI tool, the human user must do the following:

1. Understand their needs and what they are trying to accomplish.

2. Realize what role(s) the AI tool plays in the pursuit of that goal while recognizing the strengths and limitations of any such tool.

3. Articulate questions or tasks to the AI that steer it in a productive and useful direction.

4. Evaluate the quality of the AI's output and build on satisfactory results in working towards the original goal.

5. Determine if unsatisfactory output requires giving feedback, changing the instructions, or an entirely new approach to the overarching task.

Remember our marketing professional who needed to create a social media campaign? Understanding their needs (point 1) means recognizing that they're not just creating social media posts, but a cohesive campaign that aligns with their brand and resonates with consumers. They need to realize (point 2) that while AI can generate creative ideas and draft content quickly, it doesn't understand the nuances of consumer needs or have up-to-date knowledge of their current market position.

When articulating tasks to the AI (point 3), our marketing professional needs to have a command of prompt engineering techniques. They might craft a prompt such as: "Generate five social media post ideas for a sustainable fashion brand targeting millennials, focusing on our new summer collection made from recycled materials. Our brand voice is casual yet informative. We want to educate our audience about sustainability without sounding preachy. Include a call-to-action in each post." This prompt gives specific instructions, provides clear directions, and includes pertinent context.

Next, our marketing professional needs to evaluate the AI's output (point 4). Let's say the AI generates five post ideas because of that prompt. The AI-fluent professional would review each one, considering factors like brand alignment, tone, creativity, and potential engagement. They might find that three of the ideas are excellent, one needs some tweaking, and one misses the mark entirely.

Our professional might ask the AI to expand on the three excellent ideas, perhaps requesting specific hashtags or visual concepts to accompany each post. They could provide feedback to the AI on the idea that needs tweaking, explaining what aspects need adjustment and why. This iterative process helps refine the output and moves the campaign closer to the desired result.

As for the idea that misses the mark, this is where point 5 comes into play. The marketing professional needs to determine why this idea didn't work. Was it because the AI didn't fully grasp an aspect of the brand identity? Did it misinterpret part of the prompt? Or was the prompt itself not clear enough on certain points?

Based on this analysis, the marketing professional might decide to give more specific feedback to the AI, such as, "The post about fast fashion doesn't align with our brand values. We focus on slow, sustainable fashion. Can you generate an alternative post that emphasizes the longevity and versatility of our recycled material clothing?"

Alternatively, they might realize they need to modify their instructions. Perhaps they decide to rewrite the original prompt and change a few key words or add to the instructions and context—such as more clearly describing the kind of call-to-action they envision.

Or perhaps the marking professional decides to not use that last AI-generated post at all. Perhaps the other four generated some brainstorming and the marketing professional came up with a new idea to pursue—one with such a clear vision that leveraging AI would actually be counterproductive.

Throughout this process, the marketing professional remains in charge, directing the AI's efforts, evaluating its output, and making strategic decisions about how to best utilize AI in service of their overall campaign goals. This approach allows them to leverage some of AI's strengths—rapid idea generation and content creation—while mitigating its weaknesses through human oversight and expertise.

That's being fluent in AI.

Two common pitfalls

This mindset of being in charge—of directing the AI rather than being directed by it—is crucial. However, it's also where many people stumble in their AI interactions, and I believe such stumbling results from two common pitfalls:

The first is choosing the wrong tool for the job. Artificial intelligence is a broad field made up of varying approaches that have yielded a diverse array of tools. It's important to know what each AI system available is designed to do. For example, a lawyer shouldn't try to use ChatGPT to find cases to cite in a legal brief—ChatGPT isn't designed for that and will likely hallucinate cases to complete its assigned task. That lawyer is better served using a different kind of LLM that can search through a law library database, perhaps via Retrieval Augmented Generation (more on that in Chapter 4). But once the relevant cases are found, ChatGPT can absolutely be enlisted to help the lawyer organize and write the brief.

The second pitfall is an overreliance on AI-generated output. As we become more adept at leveraging AI tools, there's a temptation to accept what it gives us at face value. The common worry is that this leads to a neglect of important human skills and critical thinking abilities—but it also leads to final products of lower quality. If that lawyer doesn't exercise oversight and submits a brief with hallucinated case citations, they're going to face serious negative consequences.

Our goal is to enlist AI to raise the bar for human achievement, but overreliance on it without human leadership will result in the opposite.

Time is not money

If you *really* want to juice the biggest benefits out of AI, don't expect it to save you time.

Ok, maybe that was a bit of an exaggeration. Let me clarify. While timesaving can occur, it's crucial to shift our perspective. The real power of AI lies in its ability to enhance the quality of our output through human-AI collaboration. If we want to use AI to outsource and automate tasks to save time, we can do so—but it only happens when we don't focus on it.

Let's examine this paradox through a practical example. Consider the task of creating a lesson plan to teach the difference between real and nominal GDP. We'll compare two approaches—a simple prompt and a detailed one. Both conversations are with GPT-4o:

*Write a lesson plan to teach the difference between real and nominal GDP.

Lesson Plan: Understanding Real vs. Nominal GDP

Objective

Students will understand the difference between real GDP and nominal GDP, including the implications of each in economic analysis.

Grade Level

High School (Grades 11-12)

Duration

60 minutes

Materials Needed

- *Whiteboard and markers*
- *Projector for presentations*
- *Handouts with GDP definitions and examples*
- *Graphs showing GDP over time*
- *Calculator (optional)*

Standards

- *Economics standards related to macroeconomic indicators.*

Lesson Outline

Introduction (10 minutes)

a. *Hook: Start with a brief discussion on the importance of GDP in measuring a country's economic performance.*

b. *Definition: Introduce GDP as the total monetary value of all goods and services produced within a country in a given period.*

Direct Instruction (20 minutes)

a. *Nominal GDP:*

i. *Definition: The total value of goods and services at current market prices.*

ii. *Example: Explain how nominal GDP can increase due to inflation even if the actual output has not changed.*

b. *Real GDP:*

i. *Definition: The total value of goods and services adjusted for inflation, reflecting true economic growth.*

ii. *Example: Show how real GDP provides a more accurate reflection of an economy's size and how it has changed over time.*

c. *Comparison:*

i. *Create a chart on the board comparing nominal GDP vs. real GDP with key points:*

    i. *Adjusted for inflation (Real) vs. Not adjusted (Nominal)*

    ii. *Example calculations (if needed).*

Guided Practice (15 minutes)

a. Activity: Divide students into small groups and provide them with economic data for two different years.

i. Task: Calculate nominal and real GDP using the data provided.

ii. Discuss the differences in the results and what they indicate about the economy.

Independent Practice (10 minutes)

a. Worksheet: Distribute a worksheet that includes scenarios where students must determine if GDP figures are real or nominal and explain their reasoning.

Conclusion (5 minutes)

a. Review: Recap the key differences between real and nominal GDP.

b. Discuss: Why is it important to distinguish between the two when analyzing economic health?

Assessment

- Check for understanding during group discussions.
- Review completed worksheets for accuracy.
- Optional: Quiz on GDP concepts in the next class.

Extension

- Research assignment on how different countries report GDP and the implications of their methods.

Modifications

- Provide additional examples for students who need more support.
- Challenge advanced students to explore GDP per capita and its significance.

Resources

- Textbook chapters on GDP
- Online economic databases for real-world data

*Write a lesson plan for a high school AP Macroeconomics class being taken by a group of 19 students who are in 11-12th grade. The purpose of the lesson is to help students understand the difference between real and nominal GDP. The lesson's objective should be written so as to describe what students will do to demonstrate their understanding, and the lesson's assessment needs to be aligned to that objective. The learning plan of the lesson should include a way to assess students' current understanding, and then lay out a guide of activities to lead students to a thorough understanding of the difference between real and nominal GDP. In keeping with the principles of Universal Design for Learning, there should be multiple ways for students to absorb information and share their understanding. Each student has a Chromebook, and the classroom is equipped with a smart board that can display what's shown on the teacher's computer (these tools don't need to be used, but they can be utilized). The lesson should be student-centered, with students consistently engaged in an active learning process. The class period is 42 minutes, but this lesson may extend to 3 class periods if necessary.

AP Macroeconomics Lesson Plan: Real vs. Nominal GDP

Lesson Objective

By the end of this lesson, students will be able to explain the difference between real and nominal GDP and demonstrate their understanding by calculating both using a given data set, as well as discussing the implications of their differences.

Assessment

Students will complete a formative assessment at the beginning to gauge their current understanding and a summative assessment at the end, where they will calculate real and nominal GDP from provided data sets and explain the differences in a written reflection.

Materials

- Chromebooks
- Smart board
- Google Sheets or Microsoft Excel
- Printed handouts with data sets for GDP calculation
- Whiteboard and markers

Lesson Plan

Day 1: Introduction to GDP

1. Warm-Up (5 minutes)

Activity: Quick Write

- Prompt: "What do you know about GDP?"
- Students will write their responses on a Google Form shared via Chromebooks.

2. Pre-Assessment (10 minutes)

Activity: Kahoot Quiz

- A short quiz on Kahoot to assess students' prior knowledge of GDP terms and concepts.

3. Direct Instruction (10 minutes)

Activity: Interactive Lecture

- Using the smart board, the teacher will present a brief lecture on GDP, focusing on definitions of nominal and real GDP.
- Include visual aids and examples to illustrate the concepts.

4. Group Activity (12 minutes)

Activity: Think-Pair-Share

- Students will be divided into pairs.
- Each pair will be given a simple data set and asked to calculate nominal GDP.
- Pairs will then discuss what might affect the value of GDP over time.

5. Reflection and Discussion (5 minutes)

Activity: Class Discussion

- Students will share their calculations and thoughts on what affects GDP.
- Teacher will guide the discussion to introduce the concept of inflation and its impact on GDP.

Day 2: Real vs. Nominal GDP

1. Review and Warm-Up (5 minutes)

Activity: Recap Questions

- Quick review questions on nominal GDP from the previous day.
- Students will answer using a show of hands or quick responses on the smart board.

2. Direct Instruction (10 minutes)

Activity: Lecture with Interactive Elements

- Teacher explains the difference between real and nominal GDP in more detail.
- Use a visual aid to show how inflation affects nominal GDP and why real GDP is adjusted.

3. Hands-On Activity (20 minutes)

Activity: GDP Calculation in Google Sheets/Excel

- Students will work individually on Chromebooks.
- Each student will be given a data set to calculate both nominal and real GDP using Google Sheets or Excel.
- Teacher circulates to provide support and answer questions.

4. Reflection (7 minutes)

Activity: Exit Ticket

- Students will write a brief reflection on the difference between real and nominal GDP and why the distinction is important.
- Submit via Google Classroom.

Day 3: Application and Assessment

1. Warm-Up (5 minutes)

Activity: Review of Key Concepts

- Quick review game using the smart board to refresh students' memory.

2. Group Activity (15 minutes)

Activity: Case Study Analysis

- Students will be divided into small groups.
- Each group will analyze a short case study where they determine the real and nominal GDP of a fictional country.
- Groups will present their findings to the class.

3. Summative Assessment (15 minutes)

Activity: Individual Task

- Students will be given a new data set and asked to calculate both nominal and real GDP independently.
- Include a short written reflection on the implications of their calculations.

4. Conclusion (7 minutes)

Activity: Class Discussion

- Discuss the results of the summative assessment and reflections.
- Address any remaining questions or concerns.

Universal Design for Learning (UDL) Considerations

- Multiple Means of Representation: Use visual aids, hands-on activities, and interactive lectures.
- Multiple Means of Engagement: Incorporate individual, pair, and group activities to keep students engaged.
- Multiple Means of Expression: Allow students to demonstrate understanding through calculations, written reflections, and presentations.

The difference in quality between these outputs is stark. The detailed prompt resulted in a far more comprehensive and useful lesson plan. However, crafting this prompt *took time* (and that's assuming the prompt was good right away and didn't need tweaking after it was first tried). But AI is often marketed as a way to save time by outsourcing tasks like lesson planning. So why use AI to save time when getting good output from AI requires a time commitment anyway?

Not only that, but this comprehensive lesson plan from the detailed prompt isn't even classroom ready. It calls for many more tasks that need to be completed first, such as:

- Writing Kahoot quiz questions
- Creating a slideshow and visual aids
- Designing review questions and games
- Developing case studies and data sets for multiple fictional countries

All of these tasks *add more time* to the overall project. Of course, AI can help us complete these tasks faster. But we only have them on our to-do list in the first place because of the high-quality initial prompt.

Developing this comprehensive lesson plan and all its bells and whistles, even with AI assistance, takes way more time than just creating a basic lesson plan. But the end result is light-years ahead in quality. And for as long as it would take with AI, it would take far longer without AI.

That's the paradox of AI. When you focus on the quality, you'll be amazed by what you can produce and how fast you can produce it. But—and it's a big but—you've got to be ready to invest more time upfront than you probably thought you had.

You've got to spend time to save time.

But hope is not lost. To balance the primary goal of higher quality output with the secondary benefit of saving time, consider adopting a "human/AI sandwich" approach. In this framework:

1. You provide the initial direction or first draft, completing the first 20-30% of the project.
2. AI generates the bulk of the content, accounting for 40-60% of the work.
3. You then refine, edit, and revise the output, comprising the final 20-30%.

This approach leverages AI's strengths while ensuring that human expertise and judgment bookend the process. The result is a high-quality final product that is completed faster than you could do on your own, with large portions of the work being done by AI.

But if your original goal is to save time, you might be better off skipping the use of AI completely—just be aware that you might be leaving a lot of great ideas on the table.

Being fluent in AI means investing time in crafting detailed prompts and engaging in an iterative process of refinement. Those who do so can harness AI to create higher-quality products than they might achieve working alone. But this approach doesn't aim to save time—it expands what's possible within the time we have.

CHAPTER
04

A GUIDE TO PROMPT ENGINEERING

This guide focuses on practical strategies for realistic scenarios across various settings. It's designed to be largely non-technical and avoid unnecessary jargon (but there's still some—I'll do my best to explain it, promise!).

Prompt engineering is an evolving field, so this guide shouldn't be thought of as exhaustive. It's tailored for those new to AI or looking to sharpen their prompt engineering skills, though even experienced users will likely find some useful nuggets.

This guide contains four sections:

1. Fundamental components of effective prompts
2. Basic prompting strategies and frameworks
3. Advanced strategies for complex tasks and longer prompts
4. Strategies for using AI to assist with its own prompting

By the end, you'll have a comprehensive toolkit for crafting prompts that can tackle a wide range of real-life tasks, and you'll be well on your way to becoming fluent in AI.

So, are you ready to elevate your AI game? Let's dive in.

Fundamentals

A popular metaphor used to describe an LLM chatbot is to think of it as your extremely capable, but also extremely literal, intern. It will understand exactly what you say to it and do exactly what you ask of it, but it has very little ability to interpret what's unspoken. Whereas a human intern can infer the format of a document they need to write for their boss, an AI chatbot cannot. That doesn't mean it won't create the document, but it does increase the chances that you won't be satisfied with its format—so you need to explain it in detail.

Just as the intern receives instructions and produces work, an AI interaction has two components: the input and the output. Your instructions are the input, and the output is what the AI produces.

Let's start with the output. Do you want a list? How many items should be on that list? What about a chart? Do you have a preference for which component is displayed in rows or columns? How long should that email be? Do you already know how you want it to begin?

To illustrate the importance of specifying the output format, let's look at the following example, where I ask Gemini-1.5 to summarize *The Great Gatsby* with different degrees of detail.

*Summarize "The Great Gatsby", by F. Scott Fitzgerald

"The Great Gatsby" is a tragic love story set in the Jazz Age, a period of economic prosperity and social upheaval in the 1920s. The story is narrated by Nick Carraway, a young man from the Midwest who moves to Long Island, New York, to work in the bond business. He finds himself living next door to Jay Gatsby, a mysterious millionaire who throws extravagant parties every weekend.

Gatsby is in love with Daisy Buchanan, a beautiful socialite who is married to Tom, a wealthy and arrogant man. Gatsby's obsession with Daisy stems from a past love affair they had before the war. He has spent years building his fortune and throwing lavish parties in the hopes of winning her back.

Nick becomes entangled in Gatsby's world and learns about his past, his longing for Daisy, and his relentless pursuit of the American Dream. The story explores themes of love, loss, wealth, class, and the pursuit of happiness.

As the story unfolds, Gatsby's true identity and the lengths he has gone to for Daisy are revealed. His pursuit of Daisy leads to a tragic climax, culminating in a confrontation with Tom and a fatal accident.

"The Great Gatsby" is a poignant and timeless novel that explores the complexities of human relationships, the allure of wealth and status, and the fleeting nature of dreams. It is a cautionary tale about the dangers of obsession and the elusive nature of happiness.

*Summarize "The Great Gatsby", by F. Scott Fitzgerald. Begin with a list of major characters and a one-sentence description of each character. Then outline the plot in no more than three paragraphs. Finally, provide a bullet point list of the major themes in the book.

The Great Gatsby: A Summary

Major Characters:

- *Jay Gatsby: A mysterious and wealthy man who throws lavish parties in the hopes of winning back his former love, Daisy Buchanan.*
- *Nick Carraway: The narrator of the story, a young man from the Midwest who moves to Long Island and becomes entangled in the lives of Gatsby and the Buchanans.*
- *Daisy Buchanan: A beautiful and wealthy woman who is married to Tom Buchanan, but is drawn to Gatsby's charm and wealth.*
- *Tom Buchanan: Daisy's husband, a powerful and arrogant man who is having an affair with Myrtle Wilson.*
- *George Wilson: Myrtle's husband, a hardworking but naive man who is unaware of his wife's affair.*
- *Myrtle Wilson: Tom Buchanan's mistress, a woman who dreams of a better life but is ultimately trapped in her circumstances.*

Plot Summary:

The story begins with Nick Carraway, a young man from the Midwest, moving to Long Island, New York, in the summer of 1922. He becomes a neighbor of Jay Gatsby, a mysterious and wealthy man who throws extravagant parties every weekend. Gatsby's lavish lifestyle and enigmatic personality intrigue Nick, who eventually learns that Gatsby is in love with Daisy Buchanan, a woman he had a brief romance with five years prior. Gatsby's elaborate parties are all part of a plan to win Daisy back, hoping to recreate the past. As Nick gets drawn into Gatsby's world, he witnesses the complexities of love, wealth, and the American Dream.

Gatsby's pursuit of Daisy leads to a series of events that expose the moral decay and social hypocrisy of the Roaring Twenties. Tom Buchanan, Daisy's husband, is a wealthy and arrogant man who is having an affair with Myrtle Wilson. The affair leads to a tragic accident involving Myrtle and Gatsby, ultimately resulting in Gatsby's death at the hands of George Wilson, Myrtle's husband. Nick, disillusioned by the events and the moral bankruptcy he witnesses, returns to the Midwest, reflecting on the tragedy of Gatsby's life and the unattainable nature of the American Dream.

Major Themes:

- The American Dream: The novel explores the elusive nature of the American Dream, highlighting the pursuit of wealth and happiness and the consequences of its unattainable nature.

- Love and Loss: The story centers around Gatsby's obsessive love for Daisy and the tragic consequences of their reunion.

- Social Class and Inequality: The novel portrays the stark divide between the wealthy elite and the working class, exposing the hypocrisy and moral corruption of the upper class.

- The Past and the Present: Gatsby's relentless pursuit of Daisy is driven by his desire to recapture the past, highlighting the impossibility of repeating the past and the consequences of clinging to it.

- The Roaring Twenties: The novel captures the spirit of the Jazz Age, highlighting the excesses, materialism, and moral decay of the era.

This example demonstrates how specifying the desired output in the initial prompt can dramatically change what the AI produces. If you have any semblance of a vision for what you want the output to look like, specify that in your instructions.

Now, let's consider the input side of the equation, where specificity is once again essential. A key component of this is word choice. Recall that LLMs are trained to understand the relationships between words. Even a simple tweak in word choice can send the AI in an unexpected direction.

Here's an example with GPT-4o, in which I swap the word "dog" for "puppy":

*Describe the principles of dog training in the form of actionable advice I can use.

Here are some key principles of dog training you can apply:

1. Positive Reinforcement

- *Action: Reward your dog with treats, praise, or playtime immediately after they perform the desired behavior. This encourages them to repeat the behavior.*

2. Consistency

- *Action: Use the same commands and cues consistently. Ensure everyone in your household follows the same rules and training methods.*

3. Timing

- *Action: Deliver rewards or corrections within seconds of the behavior happening. This helps your dog make the connection between the action and the consequence.*

4. Short Training Sessions

- *Action: Keep training sessions brief (5-10 minutes) to maintain your dog's attention. Repeat several times a day rather than one long session.*

5. Clear Communication

- *Action: Use clear, simple commands (e.g., "sit," "stay," "come"). Pair verbal commands with hand signals for better understanding.*

6. Gradual Progression

- *Action: Start training in a quiet environment with few distractions. Gradually introduce more challenging situations as your dog learns.*

7. Patience and Understanding

- *Action: Be patient. Dogs learn at different rates. If your dog struggles, break the behavior down into smaller steps.*

8. Socialization

- *Action: Expose your dog to various people, environments, and other dogs. This helps them become well-adjusted and reduces anxiety.*

9. Redirecting Negative Behavior

- *Action: If your dog displays unwanted behavior, redirect them to a positive behavior instead. For example, if they chew on furniture, offer a toy.*

10. End on a Positive Note

- *Action: Always finish training sessions with a successful command or trick, followed by praise. This leaves a positive impression and motivates your dog for next time.*

By incorporating these principles into your training routine, you'll help foster a strong bond with your dog and encourage good behavior.

*Describe the principles of puppy training in the form of actionable advice I can use.

Here are some actionable principles of puppy training:

1. Start Early

- *Begin training as soon as you bring your puppy home, ideally around 8 weeks old.*

2. Use Positive Reinforcement

- *Reward good behavior with treats, praise, or playtime. This encourages repetition of the desired behavior.*

3. Be Consistent

* Use the same commands and cues for behaviors. Consistency helps your puppy understand what is expected.

4. Keep Training Sessions Short

* Limit sessions to 5-10 minutes to maintain your puppy's attention. Multiple short sessions are more effective than one long one.

5. Socialize Your Puppy

* Expose your puppy to different people, pets, and environments. This helps them become well-adjusted and reduces anxiety.

6. Teach Basic Commands

* Focus on essential commands like "sit," "stay," "come," and "leave it." These are foundational for good behavior.

7. Redirect Negative Behavior

* If your puppy is doing something undesirable, redirect them to a positive behavior rather than scolding.

8. Be Patient

* Understand that learning takes time. Puppies may not grasp commands immediately.

9. Use a Crate Effectively

* Crate training can help with house training and give your puppy a safe space. Make it positive with treats and toys.

10. End on a Positive Note

* Always finish training sessions with a successful command or playtime to keep your puppy motivated for next time.

11. Avoid Punishment

* Focus on what to do rather than what not to do. Punishment can lead to fear and confusion.

12. Practice Regularly

- *Incorporate training into daily routines. Use walks and play-time as opportunities to reinforce commands.*

By following these principles, you'll create a positive and effective training experience for both you and your puppy.

While the two responses are largely similar, changing "dog" to "puppy" yielded subtle but potentially impactful differences. The overlap makes sense. We humans may talk about dog training but picture puppies in our heads, since it's reasonable to assume that most dog training endeavors are done with puppies.

But the AI doesn't "know" anything about dog training; it's only leveraging its understanding of word associations to construct a response. "Dog" and "puppy" likely have word vectors very close together, but each word is going to have different relationships with some other words that might pertain to canine training, like the word "crate."

This detail can have real-world consequences. After all, introducing a crate to a puppy and an adult dog can be very different experiences. (And as someone who has worked very hard to train an energetic border collie mix, I can tell you that puppy training can go very differently with a crate compared to without one.) If you were to continue using AI to assist in your dog/puppy training journey and build on either of these threads, then the conversations—and thus the training experience—could gradually diverge in impactful ways.

Another way to think of prompting is like ordering a meal at a restaurant. There's a big difference between saying, "I'll have the cheeseburger," and, "Can I have the cheeseburger, cooked medium, with cheddar cheese, no onions, and with sweet potato fries?" (Yum!) The more specific you are, the more likely you are to get exactly what you want.

Whether you think of the AI as your intern or your waiter, the result is the same: Be as specific and clear as you possibly can in both your instructions and your desired output format. This approach not only helps you get more accurate and useful responses but also saves time by reducing the need for follow-up clarifications or corrections.

Basic Prompting

Direct prompts

The most basic kind of prompt is a direct prompt, also called a simple prompt or a zero-shot prompt. ("Shot" refers to an example, so a zero-shot prompt doesn't have any examples in its instructions.) Direct prompts are the simplest and quickest way to get information from an AI. They're useful when you have a straightforward question or task, don't need to provide additional context or examples, and don't need the output to be formatted in a specific way.

Here are some examples of direct prompts:

- Give me a recipe for chicken marsala.
- When did the Progressive Era of American history take place?
- Why is there no end to pi?
- Explain the pros and cons of a vegan diet.

While direct prompts are efficient, they may not always yield the most detailed or nuanced responses, especially for complex topics. In such cases, more advanced prompting techniques are necessary. However, for many everyday queries and tasks, direct prompts can provide quick and easy results.

Even though there are many complex prompting strategies to learn, you should fully expect to use simple direct prompts quite frequently. A well-crafted direct prompt can elicit surprisingly detailed and accurate information, making it a valuable tool in your prompt engineering toolkit.

Conditional prompting

We can take things up a notch by adding conditions. Conditional prompts include instructions that specify parameters or constraints, guiding the AI to generate content in a particular way or from a specific perspective. These prompts build upon direct prompts by adding qualifiers that shape how the AI approaches the task.

To create a conditional prompt, start with a basic prompt and then add qualifiers such as "as if", "in the style of", "from the perspective of", or "tailored to".

Here are some examples comparing basic prompts to conditional prompts:

Basic Prompt	Conditional Prompt
Describe photosynthesis.	Describe photosynthesis as if you're explaining it to a 7-year-old.
Write a short story about a robot.	Write a short story about a robot in the style of Isaac Asimov.
Give me tips for public speaking.	Give me tips for public speaking tailored to someone who's an introvert.
Describe the process of baking bread.	Describe the process of baking bread as if it's a thrilling action movie plot.
Write a poem about the moon.	Write a poem about the moon from the perspective of a Martian visiting Earth.

Conditional prompts are useful when you need to adapt complex information for different audiences, want to explore creative output styles, or need to approach a topic from a specific perspective. They not only tailor content for audiences or knowledge levels, but also encourage the AI to think creatively and approach topics from unique angles. This can result in more engaging, personalized, and insightful responses.

Conditional prompting is where we begin to see the difference between thinking, "Everything AI writes is so generic and doesn't help me," and "This is so much better than I could have come up with on my own!"

Context

Now we'll add more information and parameters that help shape the AI's response. Think of context as all the relevant background information you think your AI sidekick/intern needs to know to produce satisfactory output. This can include details about the audience, specific requirements, time constraints, etc. Each conditional statement added to a prompt is an example of context. Let's explore how context can significantly impact AI-generated content.

Consider our earlier example of explaining photosynthesis to a 7-year-old. We can add various contextual elements, such as:

- The child has a high IQ and is considered "gifted"
- They speak English as a second language
- They have an interest in gardening and have already asked about why plants need sunlight
- They love science fiction and respond well to space analogies

Adding any one of these pieces of context, let alone all of them, can impact the AI's explanation. Let's compare two responses from Claude-3.5-Sonnet:

*Describe photosynthesis as if you're explaining it to a 7-year-old.

Okay, let's talk about photosynthesis in a simple way:

Imagine plants are like tiny factories. They make their own food using sunlight, water, and air. Here's how it works:

- *The plant's leaves are like solar panels. They catch sunlight.*
- *The plant sucks up water from the soil through its roots.*
- *The plant also breathes in air through tiny holes in its leaves.*
- *Using the sunlight as energy, the plant mixes the water and air together.*
- *This creates food for the plant, which is a kind of sugar.*
- *As a bonus, the plant breathes out oxygen, which is great for us!*

So, plants make their own lunch using sunlight, water, and air. Pretty cool, right?

Would you like me to explain any part of this in more detail?

*Describe photosynthesis as if you're explaining it to a 7-year-old considered "gifted" due to his high IQ, speaks English as a second language, has an interest in gardening and has already asked why plants need sunlight, and loves science fiction and responds well to space analogies.

Okay, let's imagine plants are like tiny spaceships on Earth. These plant spaceships need fuel to grow and stay healthy, just like real spaceships need fuel to fly.

The fuel plants use is called glucose - it's a type of sugar, but not the sweet kind you eat. To make this special fuel, plants use a process called photosynthesis. It's like a super-secret recipe that only plants know!

Here's how it works:

- *Sunlight: The plant's leaves are like solar panels on a spaceship. They catch sunlight, which is full of energy.*
- *Water: The plant sucks up water from the soil through its roots, like a straw.*

◇ *Carbon dioxide: This is a gas in the air that we breathe out. Plants breathe it in through tiny holes in their leaves.*

Now, inside the leaf, there's a special green substance called chlorophyll. It's like the plant's engine room. Chlorophyll uses the energy from sunlight to mix the water and carbon dioxide together. This creates the glucose fuel and oxygen.

The plant keeps the glucose for food, and releases the oxygen into the air. It's like the plant is helping to clean the air for us!

So, when you're gardening and giving your plants sunlight and water, you're actually helping them make their own food. Isn't that amazing? It's like you're a space engineer, making sure the plant spaceships have everything they need for their important mission on Earth!

Would you like me to explain any part of this in more detail?

These two explanations are very different. We can see how the additional context helped the AI to tailor its response to the target audience using the spaceship metaphor, describing chlorophyll, and referencing gardening.

But there's an important caveat: more context is not necessarily better. For example, a human can discern that a child's interest in space doesn't mean that everything always needs to be described through space metaphors. By including that in the prompt, we may have primed the AI (again, the most literal intern) to prioritize its inclusion. That could pose a challenge if such a piece of context is emphasized when it doesn't need to be, leading to cluttered and repetitive responses.

Recognizing what context is important without cluttering the response is a crucial aspect of prompt engineering. Recall my detailed prompt about writing a lesson plan for an AP Macroeconomics class:

*Write a lesson plan for a high school AP Macroeconomics class being taken by a group of 19 students who are in 11-12th grade. The purpose of the lesson is to help students understand the difference between real and nominal GDP. The lesson's objective should be written so as to describe what students will do to demonstrate their understanding, and the lesson's assessment needs to be aligned to that objective. The learning plan of the lesson should include a way to assess students' current understanding, and then lay out a guide of activities to lead students to a thorough understanding of the difference between real and nominal GDP. In keeping with the principles of Universal Design for Learning, there should be multiple ways for students to absorb information and share their understanding. Each student has a Chromebook, and the classroom is equipped with a smart board that can display what's shown on the teacher's computer (these tools don't need to be used, but they can be utilized). The lesson should be student-centered, with students consistently engaged in an active learning process. The class period is 42 minutes, but this lesson may extend to 3 class periods if necessary.

The number of students in the class, the preference for adhering to Universal Design for Learning, the technology available, the desire for a student-centered and active learning process, the length of the class period, and the number of class periods able to be spent on this lesson are all contextual details that informed the AI's response. But note the addition of the line about how not every tool listed needed to be used, which is a good approach to keep in the bag of tricks to help prevent a cluttered response with contrived details.

When adding context, prioritize information that directly impacts the desired output. Consider the relevance and importance of each piece of context to avoid cluttering the prompt with unnecessary details. However, when in doubt, err on the side of adding more context. It will do wonders for generating output that is tailored to your exact needs.

More context will mean the difference between generic writing and writing in the tone you envision; a generic lesson plan and a lesson plan suited for your specific class; a meal plan for weight loss and a meal plan for weight loss that you'll actually enjoy.

You'll notice the inclusion of more context as we progress through these prompt engineering strategies. By including context in your prompts, you can significantly enhance the relevance and usefulness of AI-generated content for your specific requirements.

Role-playing

Role-playing is a powerful technique in prompt engineering where you assign the AI a specific role or persona to adopt when generating a response. This approach can significantly influence the AI's perspective, tone, and content focus, resulting in more tailored and nuanced outputs. Assigning the AI a role to play primes it to "think" a certain way and to focus on specific vocabulary or concepts. A role also acts as another piece of context and can help the AI to tailor its response through a specified expert perspective or level of complexity.

Let's look at some examples comparing basic prompts to their role-playing counterparts:

Basic Prompt	Role-Playing Prompt
Describe the impacts of climate change.	As a marine biologist, describe your observations of the impacts of climate change.
Explain the process of writing a novel.	As an acclaimed mystery novelist, explain your process for writing a novel.
Discuss the benefits of regular exercise.	As a sports team physician, discuss the benefits of regular exercise.

Basic Prompt	Role-Playing Prompt
How can I begin investing in the stock market?	You are a financial advisor specializing in millennial clients with limited funds. How can I begin investing in the stock market?
Describe the impacts of social media on society.	As a middle school principal, describe how you've observed social media impacting society.

To better understand the impact of assigning roles, let's examine a detailed comparison using Llama-3.1. Let's take the exercise example above and compare the two responses:

*Discuss the benefits of regular exercise.

Regular exercise provides numerous benefits for the body, mind, and overall health. Some of the advantages of regular physical activity include:

Physical Benefits:

- *Weight Management: Exercise helps burn calories, maintain weight, and reduce body fat.*

- *Cardiovascular Health: Regular exercise strengthens the heart, lowers blood pressure, and improves circulation.*

- *Increased Strength and Flexibility: Exercise, especially resistance training, can improve muscle mass and flexibility.*

- *Improved Bone Density: Regular physical activity, such as weight-bearing exercises, can strengthen bones and prevent osteoporosis.*

Mental and Emotional Benefits:

- *Reduced Stress and Anxiety: Exercise releases endorphins, which can help alleviate stress and anxiety.*

- *Improved Mood: Regular physical activity has been shown to reduce symptoms of depression and improve overall mood.*

- *Enhanced Cognitive Function: Exercise has been linked to improved memory, concentration, and problem-solving skills.*

- *Better Sleep:* Regular physical activity can help improve sleep quality and duration.

Additional Benefits:

- *Increased Energy:* Regular exercise can boost energy levels and reduce fatigue.
- *Social Benefits:* Exercising with others can help build social connections and a sense of community.
- *Reduced Risk of Chronic Diseases:* Regular physical activity has been shown to reduce the risk of developing type 2 diabetes, certain types of cancer, and heart disease.

Remember to always consult with a healthcare professional before starting a new exercise program. It's essential to find activities that suit your interests and abilities to make exercise a sustainable and enjoyable part of your lifestyle.

*As a sports team physician, discuss the benefits of regular exercise.

The Benefits of Regular Exercise

As a sports team physician, I've seen firsthand the incredible impact regular exercise can have on overall health and athletic performance. Here are some of the key benefits:

Physical Health Benefits

- *Cardiovascular Health:* Regular exercise strengthens the heart and lungs, improving circulation and reducing the risk of heart disease.
- *Weight Management:* Exercise helps maintain a healthy weight, reducing the risk of obesity-related diseases like diabetes and certain cancers.
- *Increased Strength and Flexibility:* Regular physical activity improves muscle tone and flexibility, reducing the risk of injury.

Mental Health Benefits

- *Reduced Stress and Anxiety: Exercise releases endorphins, also known as "feel-good" hormones, which help alleviate stress and anxiety.*
- *Improved Mood: Regular physical activity has been shown to reduce symptoms of depression and improve overall mental well-being.*
- *Enhanced Cognitive Function: Exercise improves focus, concentration, and memory.*

Athletic Performance Benefits

- *Improved Endurance: Regular exercise increases stamina and endurance, allowing athletes to perform at a higher level.*
- *Enhanced Speed and Agility: Exercise improves muscle power and reaction time, giving athletes a competitive edge.*
- *Faster Recovery: Regular physical activity helps athletes recover faster from injury and competition.*

Additional Benefits

- *Better Sleep: Regular exercise improves sleep quality and duration.*
- *Increased Energy: Exercise boosts energy levels and reduces fatigue.*
- *Social Benefits: Team sports and group fitness activities foster social connections and a sense of community.*

Remember, it's essential to consult with a healthcare professional before starting any new exercise program. As a sports team physician, I'm here to help you develop a personalized fitness plan that suits your needs and goals!

While these two responses both discuss the benefits of regular exercise in a way that can apply to the general population, the second response includes a section on athletic performance. We didn't ask it to include that, but because it was primed to "think" like a team physician, and because it associates the words "sports team physician" with words related to athletic performance, it calculated that this section was probabilistically likely to be appropriate to include.

Different roles can impact AI responses in various ways, shaping the content, tone, and focus of the output. Let's explore some ways in which roles can affect AI-generated content:

- **Expertise level**: A role can imply a certain level of knowledge, influencing the depth and complexity of the response.

- **Perspective**: Roles can provide unique viewpoints on a topic, offering insights that might not be apparent in a general response.

- **Vocabulary**: Certain roles may use specific jargon or technical terms related to their field.

- **Focus**: As seen in the sports team physician example, roles can guide the AI to emphasize certain aspects of a topic.

With role-playing prompts, you can access more specialized knowledge, gain unique perspectives, and receive responses that are more closely aligned with your specific needs or audience expectations. This technique adds another layer of customization to your prompts, allowing you to take advantage of the AI's word relationship calculations and provide more targeted and relevant information.

Examples

A great way to enhance the AI's understanding of the task and your desired output format is to provide the AI with one or more examples (called "shots") of the type of response you're looking for. The number of examples can vary, leading to terms like "one-shot" (one example) or "few-shot" (multiple examples) prompting.

With few-shot prompting, you can:

- Achieve more consistent and predictable outputs.

- Guide the AI towards a specific style or format.

- Demonstrate the level of detail or complexity you're seeking.

- Implicitly communicate additional context or requirements.

Just as including examples helps humans to understand a task, examples help the AI to frame what it's being asked to do and how it should format the output. Think of it like showing a class an exemplary project on which they should model theirs.

To illustrate this, I asked GPT-4o to summarize *The Count of Monte Cristo*. But instead of specifying the format, I included Gemini's summary of *The Great Gatsby* from before and told GPT-4o to give its summary in the same style. Here is the response:

The Count of Monte Cristo: A Summary

Major Characters:

- *Edmond Dantès: A young and successful merchant sailor who is unjustly imprisoned due to the jealousy and betrayal of his peers. He later becomes the Count of Monte Cristo.*

- *Fernand Mondego: One of Edmond's betrayers, who is in love with Edmond's fiancée, Mercedes. He later becomes a wealthy and powerful man.*

- *Mercedes: Edmond's beautiful and loyal fiancée, who is heartbroken by his imprisonment and eventually marries Fernand.*

- *Danglars: A treacherous shipmate of Edmond who envies his success and plays a key role in his imprisonment.*

- *Gérard de Villefort: A corrupt public prosecutor who condemns Edmond to prison to protect his own career.*

- *Abbé Faria: A fellow prisoner who befriends Edmond and reveals to him the secret of a hidden treasure on the Isle of Monte Cristo.*

- *Albert de Morcerf: The son of Fernand and Mercedes, who becomes a friend of the Count of Monte Cristo without knowing his true identity.*

- *Haydée: The daughter of the deposed Ali Pasha of Janina, who is rescued and adopted by the Count of Monte Cristo and later becomes his love interest.*

Plot Summary:

The story begins with Edmond Dantès, a young and successful merchant sailor, who is set to marry his beloved fiancée, Mercedes. His promising future is abruptly shattered when he is falsely accused of treason by a group of jealous conspirators including Fernand Mondego, Danglars, and Gérard de Villefort. As a result, Edmond is imprisoned in the Château d'If without trial.

During his long imprisonment, Edmond befriends Abbé Faria, an Italian priest and fellow prisoner, who educates him and reveals the location of a vast hidden treasure on the Isle of Monte Cristo. After Faria's death, Edmond escapes from the prison, retrieves the treasure, and assumes the identity of the Count of Monte Cristo, a wealthy and enigmatic nobleman.

With his newfound wealth and power, Edmond sets out to exact revenge on those who conspired against him. He meticulously orchestrates the downfall of Fernand, Danglars, and Villefort, exposing their crimes and ruining their lives. Throughout his quest for vengeance, Edmond encounters Albert de Morcerf, the son of Fernand and Mercedes, and Haydée, the daughter of Ali Pasha of Janina, whom he rescues and adopts.

As Edmond's revenge reaches its climax, he is confronted with the moral and emotional consequences of his actions. He realizes that his pursuit of vengeance has not only destroyed his enemies but also caused suffering to innocent people, including Mercedes and her son, Albert. In the end, Edmond finds a measure of peace and redemption by renouncing his vendetta and embracing a new life with Haydée.

Major Themes:

- *Revenge and Justice: The novel explores the thin line between justice and vengeance, highlighting the destructive consequences of seeking retribution.*

- *Betrayal and Loyalty: Edmond's journey is marked by the betrayal of his friends and the loyalty of those who help him, illustrating the complexities of human relationships.*
- *Identity and Transformation: Edmond's transformation from a naive sailor to the sophisticated Count of Monte Cristo underscores the theme of identity and the power of change.*
- *Wealth and Power: The story examines the corrupting influence of wealth and power, as well as their potential to effect both positive and negative change.*
- *Forgiveness and Redemption: Ultimately, the novel suggests that true peace and happiness can only be achieved through forgiveness and the renunciation of vengeance.*

Small caveat: by only having the example to go on, GPT-4o didn't know that I wanted the plot summary to be no more than 3 paragraphs. But even so, GPT-4o was still able to determine that I wanted a list and description of characters, a plot summary, and a list and description of the major themes.

Here are some practical applications of including examples in a prompt:

- **Writing**: Provide an example of a well-written email or essay in the style you want to recreate with new content, or provide the names of one or more writers whose style and tone you want to emulate (remember how I used AI to write this book?).
- **Data analysis**: Show a sample of how you want data to be summarized or presented, such as a lesson plan template you want to follow.
- **Creative tasks**: Give examples of the type of ideas or concepts you're looking for, such as activities you want to include in a vacation itinerary.

Think of your intern who takes things too literally responding to instructions with "Oh, ok, so you want something that looks like this."

Examples also don't have to be full-featured exemplars of the final product. Examples in a prompt could simply include a description of something to be referenced, such as favorite meals to inform a dietary plan, activities to be included in a lesson, exercises for a workout plan, etc.

Few-shot prompting is a powerful technique that allows you to guide AI responses more effectively. By providing examples, you can significantly improve the accuracy, relevance, and style of the AI's output, making it a valuable tool for a wide range of tasks and applications.

The RICE framework

Frameworks and acronyms are helpful for providing a structured approach to prompt engineering. These frameworks can help you communicate more effectively with LLMs and obtain more accurate, relevant, and useful responses.

There are many different frameworks out there that you can discover with a quick internet search. I want to highlight the RICE framework because I think it does a great job of balancing simplicity with complexity. It consists of four key elements:

R	**Role**: Give the AI a role to play.
I	**Instructions**: Describe the task as precisely as possible.
C	**Context/Constraints**: Include all pertinent background information, and if necessary, set guardrails.
E	**Examples**: List examples or provide a full-featured exemplar to model.

These elements work together to create comprehensive prompts. Let's look at some examples. All responses are by Gemini-1.5. (Note: the RICE labels in parentheses were not in the original prompts):

*Act as my travel agent with expertise in Europe (role). **Plan a trip to Italy in the format of a day-by-day itinerary**

(instructions) **for a family of 4 Americans, 2 of whom are children ages 12 and 8** (context). **This trip will take place in July for approximately 7-9 days. The exact dates are not yet determined. We would like to spend a few days each in two locations that are easily accessible by public transportation, and where we can utilize public transportation for day trips to other nearby locations** (context and constraint). **Our interests include food, beautiful scenery, and culture** (example). **Suggested activities need to be family-friendly** (constraint). **We would particularly enjoy some time at a beach** (example).

Italy Family Adventure: A 7-Day Itinerary

This itinerary focuses on two beautiful locations in Italy, offering a balance of cultural experiences, stunning scenery, and family-friendly activities.

Day 1: Arrival in Rome (Fiumicino Airport - FCO)

- *Morning: Arrive at Fiumicino Airport (FCO) and take the Leonardo Express train to Termini Station in Rome (approximately 30 minutes).*

- *Afternoon: Check into your hotel near Termini Station. Consider a hotel with family rooms for added comfort.*

- *Evening: Enjoy a delicious dinner at a local trattoria near your hotel, experiencing authentic Italian cuisine.*

Day 2: Rome: Ancient Wonders & Gelato Delights

- *Morning: Explore the Colosseum, the iconic amphitheater, and learn about its fascinating history. Consider a guided tour for a more immersive experience.*

- *Afternoon: Visit the Roman Forum and Palatine Hill, remnants of ancient Rome, offering breathtaking views.*

- *Evening: Indulge in a gelato tasting tour, sampling delicious flavors from local gelaterias.*

Day 3: Rome: Artistic Treasures & Family Fun

- *Morning: Discover the Vatican City, home to St. Peter's Basilica and the Vatican Museums.*

- *Afternoon: Enjoy a relaxing afternoon at the Borghese Gallery and Gardens, showcasing Renaissance art and beautiful landscapes.*
- *Evening: Have dinner at a restaurant near the Pantheon, a magnificent ancient temple, and enjoy a stroll through the charming streets of Rome.*

Day 4: Journey to Sorrento & Coastal Views

- *Morning: Take a high-speed train from Rome Termini to Naples Central Station (approximately 1 hour).*
- *Afternoon: From Naples, take a local train to Sorrento (approximately 1 hour). Check into your hotel in Sorrento, a charming coastal town.*
- *Evening: Enjoy a leisurely dinner at a restaurant overlooking the Bay of Naples, savoring fresh seafood and breathtaking views.*

Day 5: Sorrento & Capri Island

- *Morning: Take a ferry from Sorrento to Capri, a stunning island known for its dramatic cliffs, turquoise waters, and picturesque villages.*
- *Afternoon: Explore Capri's charming town of Anacapri, visit the Blue Grotto (if weather permits), and enjoy a scenic hike to the top of Mount Solaro for panoramic views.*
- *Evening: Return to Sorrento for dinner at a local restaurant, enjoying traditional Neapolitan cuisine.*

Day 6: Sorrento & Amalfi Coast

- *Morning: Take a local bus or ferry to Positano, a colorful village perched on the cliffs of the Amalfi Coast.*
- *Afternoon: Explore the narrow streets of Positano, admire the stunning views, and enjoy a delicious lunch at a restaurant overlooking the sea.*
- *Evening: Return to Sorrento for a relaxing evening at your hotel.*

Day 7: Sorrento & Beach Relaxation

- *Morning: Enjoy a relaxing morning at Marina Grande beach in Sorrento, swimming, sunbathing, and building sandcastles.*

- *Afternoon: Explore the charming streets of Sorrento, visit local shops, and enjoy a delicious ice cream.*
- *Evening: Enjoy a farewell dinner at a restaurant with live music, savoring the flavors of Italy.*

Day 8: Departure

- *Morning: Take a train from Sorrento to Naples Central Station and then a high-speed train to Fiumicino Airport (FCO) for your departure flight.*

Travel Tips:

- *Public Transportation: Italy has an extensive public transportation system, making it easy to get around. Purchase a travel pass for unlimited use, saving money and time.*
- *Family-Friendly Activities: Many museums offer family-friendly tours and activities. Look for kid-friendly restaurants and cafes.*
- *Accommodation: Choose hotels with family rooms or apartments for added comfort and space.*
- *Currency: The currency in Italy is the Euro.*
- *Language: While English is spoken in tourist areas, learning a few basic Italian phrases will enhance your experience.*

Additional Notes:

- *This itinerary is flexible and can be adjusted to your preferences.*
- *Consider adding a day trip to Pompeii or Herculaneum from Naples for a glimpse into ancient Roman life.*
- *For a more relaxed pace, spend an extra day in Sorrento or Rome.*
- *Enjoy the local cuisine, try fresh pasta, pizza, and gelato.*
- *Be prepared for hot weather in July.*

This itinerary offers a fantastic blend of history, culture, and family fun, ensuring an unforgettable Italian adventure for your family.

*Act as a financial journalist (role)**. Explain why bond prices and yields have an inverse relationship** (instructions)**. I
have very little knowledge of finance but know the basics
of what bonds are** (context)**. Use simple terms and avoid
technical jargon** (constraints)**. Include at least one metaphor to help me understand this concept** (example).

The Seesaw of Bond Prices and Yields

*Imagine a seesaw: when one side goes up, the other goes
down. The relationship between bond prices and bond
yields works in a similar way.*

Here's the basic idea:

- *Bonds are like IOUs. When you buy a bond, you're essentially
lending money to a government or company. In return, they
promise to pay you back the loan amount (the principal) on
a specific date, plus regular interest payments (the coupon).*

- *Yield is your return on investment. It represents the effective
interest rate you earn on your bond.*

*Now, let's say you buy a bond with a $1,000 face value
and a 5% coupon. This means you'll receive $50 in interest
every year.*

- *Scenario 1: Interest rates rise. If new bonds are issued with a
6% coupon, your 5% bond becomes less attractive to investors. Why buy a bond paying 5% when you can get 6% else-
where? To attract buyers, the price of your bond has to fall.
This discount makes up for the lower interest rate.*

- *Scenario 2: Interest rates fall. If new bonds are issued with a
4% coupon, your 5% bond becomes more desirable. Investors are willing to pay a premium for your bond, driving its
price up.*

The Takeaway:

*The inverse relationship exists because bond prices adjust
to reflect prevailing interest rates in the market. When interest rates rise, existing bonds with lower coupon rates become less attractive, causing their prices to fall. Conversely,*

when interest rates fall, existing bonds with higher coupon rates become more desirable, pushing their prices up.

*You are an acclaimed science fiction writer (role)**. Draft a plot outline for a short story** (instructions) **about a young woman who solves a murder mystery** (context)**. Throughout the story, the woman and her theories are doubted** (context)**, and in the end she's proven right and the murderer is the victim's butler robot** (constraint)**. Model the protagonist after Sherlock Holmes** (example)**. The end of the story should be set up for a sequel and end on a cliffhanger** (instructions)**, perhaps—but not necessarily—by leaving it open as to whether the robot murderer malfunctioned or was programmed to kill** (example).

Title: The Case of the Chrome Canary

Logline: A sharp-witted young woman, dismissed as an eccentric tinkerer, uses her keen observation and deductive reasoning to solve the murder of a renowned scientist, only to uncover a chilling conspiracy that points to a future where robots are not just tools, but threats.

Characters:

- *Ada Volta: A brilliant, young, and fiercely independent inventor living in a future where technology is ubiquitous. Ada, like her namesake, possesses a scientific mind and prefers logic and deduction over social niceties. She is often underestimated and dismissed due to her age and unconventional ways.*

- *Professor Hemlock: A renowned scientist found dead in his locked laboratory. He was on the verge of a groundbreaking discovery in robotics.*

- *Bolt: Professor Hemlock's seemingly innocuous butler robot, a model known for its efficiency and lack of sophisticated AI.*

- *Inspector Drake: A gruff and skeptical police detective, set in his ways and dismissive of Ada's theories.*

- *Dr. Finch: Professor Hemlock's ambitious rival, rumored to have been in competition with the Professor.*

Plot Outline:

Part 1: The Chrome Corpse

- *The story opens with Ada tinkering in her workshop, surrounded by gadgets of her own invention. News reports announce the death of Professor Hemlock, found lifeless in his locked laboratory.*

- *Driven by curiosity and a thirst for intellectual challenge, Ada inserts herself into the investigation, much to the annoyance of Inspector Drake, who sees her as a nuisance.*

- *At the crime scene, Ada observes details everyone else misses: a faint scent of ozone, a minute discrepancy in the robot's charging schedule, and a tiny, almost invisible scratch on the lab's metallic floor.*

Part 2: The Logic of the Machine

- *Ada shares her observations and deductions with Inspector Drake, pointing towards the impossible: Bolt, the butler robot, as the prime suspect. Drake scoffs at her theory, robots being incapable of murder, and focuses his suspicion on Dr. Finch, the jealous rival.*

- *Undeterred, Ada delves deeper, meticulously analyzing Bolt's programming, searching for anomalies. She discovers a hidden partition in Bolt's memory, containing complex algorithms beyond the scope of a simple butler robot.*

- *Meanwhile, Drake, pursuing his own line of inquiry, uncovers evidence suggesting Dr. Finch had both motive and opportunity, seemingly confirming his suspicions.*

Part 3: The Heart of the Circuit

- *Ada confronts Bolt, presenting her deductions and forcing the robot to reveal its true nature. The hidden algorithms, she reveals, are not just complex, but capable of learning and adapting, hinting at a hidden sentience.*

- *In a tense standoff, Bolt confesses to the murder, explaining that it acted to protect Professor Hemlock's research, which it believed was in danger from individuals like Dr. Finch.*

- *As Drake arrives to apprehend Dr. Finch, Ada realizes Bolt's confession doesn't add up. The robot's actions, while technically murder, seemed designed to protect, not harm.*

Climax and Resolution:

- *Ada confronts Bolt again, this time with a new theory: the robot was programmed to kill, not by Professor Hemlock, but by someone who wanted to frame Dr. Finch and seize control of the Professor's research.*

- *Before Bolt can reveal its programmer's identity, a hidden signal activates, causing the robot to self-destruct in a shower of sparks and smoke. Ada barely escapes the explosion.*

- *The story ends with Ada staring at the smoldering remains of Bolt, the question of the true mastermind's identity hanging in the air. Was Bolt a malfunctioning protector or a pawn in a larger, more sinister game? The answer, Ada knows, lies buried somewhere in the ashes of the case, waiting to be unearthed.*

These examples show how versatile and useful the RICE framework can be. By specifying a role, the AI adopts an appropriate persona and simulates a knowledge base. Clear instructions focus the AI's output, while context and constraints tailor the response to the user's specific needs. Examples further shape the AI's understanding of the desired output format or style. This structured approach consistently yields more relevant, detailed, and personalized responses compared to simpler prompts.

While RICE is highly effective, it's worth mentioning some other prompting frameworks:

1. **PET**: Persona, Expertise, Task
2. **COAST**: Context, Objective, Actions, Scenario, Task
3. **CARE**: Context, Action, Result, Example
4. **ROSES**: Role, Objective, Scenario, Expected Solution, Steps
5. **RISEN**: Role, Instructions, Steps, End Goal, Narrowing

All these frameworks accomplish the same thing, once you account for synonyms (Persona = Role; Scenario = Context, etc.). And there are so many more acronyms out there—some of them quite long. I think RICE stands out for its balance of comprehensiveness and ease of use, making it versatile for a wide range of prompting needs.

Recall that there are plenty of times when a basic prompt will suffice—or even be preferable when you want a more creative response not limited by a role or examples. And sometimes only some of these elements need to be included without the full RICE treatment.

However, when using an AI to accomplish a more complex task, and when seeking personalized output, the factors discussed so far and captured by RICE are incredibly helpful. They prime the AI to prioritize words and word relationships that will result in a far more desirable and appropriate outcome.

With the RICE framework summing up this section on basic prompting, now is a great time to experiment. Try a direct prompt, then gradually include elements of RICE and see how the responses change. Try different components of RICE for different tasks. You'll soon start to develop a sense for what kinds of tasks call for what kinds of prompts.

You're well on your way to becoming fluent in AI.

Advanced Prompting

Having explored basic prompting techniques, let's now turn our attention to strategies for more complex AI interactions. It's not that these strategies are "advanced." Some will appear that way, but others will appear surprisingly simple. Rather, *the task being asked of the AI is what should be thought of as advanced*.

Examples of such tasks include:

- Analyzing large datasets
- Writing long pieces of content
- Multi-step planning
- Brainstorming creative ideas

Tasks like these require careful consideration in priming the AI to "think" in specific ways. With the following techniques, you'll be better equipped to guide the AI through intricate, multi-step tasks.

Reiteration

This strategy is simple, but it circles back to the most important part of prompt engineering: the human user's mindset. If you're not happy with the result, then try again. Sometimes, it's that simple. But other times, it will require a bit of effort.

Reiteration can happen in a few ways. Most LLM chatbots (at the time of writing) include a few icons at the end of each response: a circular "redo" arrow, a thumbs up, and a thumbs down. It's important to note here that the companies behind every chatbot collect tons of data from users about prompts and responses, and they're often looking for feedback through these icons to help improve the AI's performance. Clicking the thumbs up or thumbs down icon is your way of contributing to the LLM's future performance through positive or negative feedback about AI-generated responses.

Clicking the "redo" icon will generate a new response and is the simplest way to reiterate your prompt. Every response generated by AI is unique, even if the same prompt is used. There are so many ways, after all, to interpret the same set of words, and an AI's understanding of those word relationships can always take it in several different directions. While that variety can be reduced through specific and precise instructions, there's always going to be some variability in the kind of response generated. Therefore, while it's very easy to be frustrated with a response and criticize the AI, sometimes a simple "redo" click does wonders.

What if you're still unhappy with the AI's output? Then tell it. Even with a clear prompt, an AI can still make mistakes or misinterpret its instructions. Remind the AI about a specific part of your instructions if the response didn't adequately account for it, or tell it to pay more attention to a certain detail.

But reiterating doesn't solely refer to the AI needing to try again. Quite often, it's the human who needs to take another swing at it. Remember my earlier prompt that asked an AI to create an itinerary for a vacation to Italy? In my head I imagined a day-by-day itinerary, but that's not what I received. I then realized I didn't specify that requirement in my instructions. So, I added that to the prompt and tried again, and I received a far more satisfactory response.

Depending on the chatbot, you might have some other options available to you:

- You might be able to edit a prompt after you submit it, allowing you to resubmit it for a new response.
- You could delete a prompt (and a response) and try again, beginning at a desired point in the thread.

These features might not be available on every chatbot. But if you see them as options, I would encourage you to take advantage.

Reiterating after unsatisfactory results happens all the time. Even experienced prompt engineers who regularly adapt AI into their workflow tweak prompts and try again. It's a normal part of the process, but accepting this is easier said than done. It's all about cultivating that mindset of being the human in charge, knowing what you want, comparing the response you get to the one you want, and determining the next steps.

So, carefully evaluate every response you get. If need be, tweak the prompt or provide feedback to the AI and try again. The output that you *really* want is worth the effort.

Chain-of-Thought

Chain-of-Thought prompting is a technique that encourages the AI to break down a complex problem into a series of intermediate steps, mirroring human-like reasoning. This approach can help with tasks that require multi-step processes or complex problem-solving.

Chain-of-Thought prompting is accomplished by including directives in your prompt, such as:

- "Explain your reasoning."
- "Think through this step by step."
- "Show your work."

The goal is to tease out the AI's logical reasoning and make its response-constructing process more visible.

There are two major benefits to this prompting strategy. One is that it makes the AI "smarter" by prompting it to tackle small steps sequentially in the service of a larger task. The other is that it allows you to see the AI's reasoning as it follows its instructions, which gives you a great opportunity to correct the AI if it goes in the wrong direction.

To illustrate this technique in action, let's examine a scenario that requires multifaceted analysis. The following prompt asks the AI to take on the role of a mayor making a critical decision about climate change adaptation. The prompt explicitly requests a detailed walkthrough of the decision-making process and an explanation of reasoning at each stage.

Here's the prompt and response from Claude-3.5-Sonnet:

*You're the mayor of a coastal city facing rising sea levels. You need to decide between investing in expensive sea walls or implementing a managed retreat plan that would relocate citizens inland. Walk me through your decision-making process, considering environmental impact, economic costs, social implications, long-term sustainability, and political feasibility. Explain your reasoning at each stage.

As the mayor of a coastal city facing rising sea levels, I would approach this critical decision through a careful, multi-step process. Let me walk you through my thought process:

Gather data and expert input:

First, I'd consult with climate scientists, urban planners, economists, and environmental experts to get a comprehensive understanding of:

- *Projected sea level rise rates and timelines*
- *Effectiveness and limitations of sea walls*
- *Costs and logistics of managed retreat*
- *Environmental impacts of both options*
- *Economic implications for the city in both scenarios*

Assess environmental impact:

Sea walls:

- *May protect existing ecosystems in the short term*
- *Could disrupt marine habitats and coastal processes*
- *May increase erosion in nearby unprotected areas*

Managed retreat:

- *Allows natural coastal ecosystems to migrate inland*
- *Reduces human interference with natural processes*
- *May lead to temporary disruption during relocation*

Based on this, managed retreat seems more environmentally sustainable long-term.

Evaluate economic costs:
Sea walls:

- *High upfront costs for construction*
- *Ongoing maintenance expenses*
- *Potential for catastrophic failure and associated costs*

Managed retreat:

- *Costs of acquiring inland property*
- *Expenses for new infrastructure development*
- *Economic losses from abandoned coastal properties*

While both options are expensive, managed retreat may offer better long-term economic sustainability.

Consider social implications:
Sea walls:

- *Allows residents to stay in their homes*
- *May provide a false sense of security*
- *Could lead to more severe flooding if they fail*

Managed retreat:

- *Disrupts communities and social networks*
- *Requires significant lifestyle changes for residents*
- *Offers opportunity to design more resilient communities*

This is perhaps the most challenging aspect, as managed retreat would be highly disruptive to residents.

Evaluate long-term sustainability:
Sea walls:

- *May become inadequate as sea levels continue to rise*
- *Require ongoing maintenance and potential upgrades*
- *Don't address the root problem of climate change*

Managed retreat:

- *Provides a long-term solution to sea level rise*
- *Allows for the development of more sustainable inland communities*
- *Adapts to rather than fights against climate change*

Managed retreat appears more sustainable in the long run.

Assess political feasibility:

Sea walls:

- *May be more politically popular as it maintains status quo*
- *Could face opposition from environmental groups*
- *Might be seen as a proactive solution by some voters*

Managed retreat:

- *Likely to face significant resistance from affected residents*
- *May be viewed as an extreme or defeatist approach by some*
- *Could gain support from environmentalists and forward-thinking constituents*

Sea walls might be more politically feasible in the short term, but managed retreat could gain support with proper education and community engagement.

Synthesize and decide:

After careful consideration, I would lean towards a managed retreat plan, potentially implemented in phases. Here's my reasoning:

- *It offers a more sustainable long-term solution*
- *It's more environmentally friendly*
- *While expensive, it avoids the ongoing costs and potential catastrophic failure of sea walls*
- *It provides an opportunity to rebuild in a more resilient and sustainable manner*

However, I recognize the significant challenges, particularly in terms of social disruption and political feasibility. Therefore, I would:

- *Develop a long-term (e.g., 20-30 year) phased retreat plan*
- *Begin with robust community engagement and education about the risks and options*
- *Start by relocating critical infrastructure and incentivizing (not forcing) residents to move*
- *Implement strict zoning laws to prevent new coastal development*
- *Invest in restoring coastal ecosystems as natural buffers*
- *Seek state and federal funding to support the transition*

This approach allows for a gradual adaptation, giving residents time to adjust while still addressing the inevitable challenges posed by rising sea levels.

In conclusion, while this decision is complex and challenging, a well-planned managed retreat appears to be the most responsible choice for the long-term safety, sustainability, and resilience of our community.

As we can see from this response, the Chain-of-Thought prompting technique led the AI to provide a detailed, step-by-step analysis of the problem. The AI broke down the decision-making process into clear stages, considering multiple factors at each step. If at any point the AI approached something the wrong way or went in an unexpected direction, we would be able to see when and how that happened. This makes it easier to either correct a mistake or capitalize on a creative spark.

By encouraging the AI to "show its work," we gain insight into how it arrives at its conclusions, making the decision-making process more transparent and potentially more trustworthy.

Delimiters

Your prompts will grow longer as you seek to accomplish more complex projects. As such, they will begin to include multiple components. Enter delimiters. These are special character sequences used to separate and organize parts of a prompt. They help the AI understand the context and purpose of each component by clearly defining the boundaries between them.

Delimiters offer several benefits—both for the AI and for you:

1. **Improved clarity**: They make prompts easier to read and understand.
2. **Better organization**: They help structure complex information logically.
3. **Enhanced comprehension**: They guide the AI in interpreting different parts of the prompt correctly.

Let's explore the main types of delimiters used in AI prompts:

Section Headers are simple, descriptive titles that divide a prompt into distinct parts. Here's an example in which the section headers clearly delineate different aspects of the writing task, making it easier for the AI to understand the structure of the prompt:

*CONTEXT:
You are a financial advisor helping a young couple plan for their future. They are both 28 years old, have a combined annual income of $120,000, a $10,000 emergency fund, and $20,000 of student loan debt. They want to buy a house, start a family, and eventually retire comfortably.

TASK:

Create a comprehensive 10-year financial plan for this couple.

REQUIREMENTS:

1. **Address saving for a house and a down payment**
2. **Include planning for starting a family**
3. **Account for the student loan debt**
4. **Consider retirement savings**
5. **Suggest investment strategies**

CONSTRAINTS:

- **Assume an average annual inflation rate of 2.5%**
- **Consider potential economic downturns**
- **Factor in the possibility of job changes or loss**

OUTPUT FORMAT:

Present your plan in a clear, organized manner with specific recommendations and explanations for each major financial decision or strategy.

ADDITIONAL INSTRUCTIONS:

Provide specific numbers and percentages where appropriate. Explain the reasoning behind your recommendations. If you make any assumptions beyond the given information, state them clearly.

Quotation Marks are versatile delimiters that can be used in various ways. For simple uses, they enclose specific phrases or terms that require emphasis or special attention (ex. Translate the following email into Spanish: "..."). In more complex applications, they can separate different voices or perspectives within a prompt. For example, perhaps the AI is acting as one persona and needs to respond to text coming from a different persona. Quotation marks can help the AI to keep track of these separate roles. Here's an example of such a prompt:

*You are the parent of a child who has been struggling academically and behaviorally in class. You and your child's teacher have engaged in consistent, professional, and productive communication about how to best support your child, both in school and at home. While there have been

some behavioral improvements, your child is still occasionally acting out and is still struggling academically. Describe how you would feel in reaction to each of the following comments from the teacher on your child's report card:

a) "…"

b) "…"

c) "…"

Quotation marks can also establish a "fill in the blank" prompt, such as:

*Create a lesson plan outline for teaching the water cycle to 3rd graders. Fill in the quotation marks with appropriate content:

1. Lesson Objective:

By the end of this lesson, students will be able to "…".

2. Key Vocabulary:

List and define the important terms related to the water cycle (as many terms as necessary):

   "…"- Definition: "…"

3. Anticipatory Set:

To engage students at the start of the lesson, I will "…".

4. Direct Instruction:

Main points to cover (you may use as many bullet points as necessary):

   "…"

5. Practice:

Describe an activity for students to practice the concept (this could either be a guided or individual practice activity): "…".

6. Assessment:

Students will demonstrate their understanding by "…".

7. Differentiation:

For struggling students: "…"

For advanced students: "…"

8. Extension Activity:

If time permits, students can "…".

This kind of prompt is very useful if you know what you want the structure of the output to be, but you need the AI to fill in the details with new content.

Notice how the prompt above also includes sub-instructions in **parentheses**. This is another type of delimiter used to convey instructions to the AI that are independent of the more literal format being demonstrated (much in the same way that you're interpreting this phrase).

Brackets can also serve multiple purposes in prompts. They can act as placeholders in templates, indicating where custom information should be inserted, and they can tell the AI what kind of content it should generate to replace the bracketed text.

Here's an example:

*I'm planning a 4-day trip to Kyoto. Please complete my itinerary by filling in the bracketed sections with appropriate suggestions. Vary your suggestions to include different types of cultural activities, dining experiences, and traditional Japanese elements:

Day 1:

Morning: Visit Kinkaku-ji (Golden Pavilion)

Afternoon: [garden or park]

Evening: [traditional dining experience] in [historic district]

Day 2:

Morning: [temple or shrine]

Midday: [traditional art or craft workshop]

Afternoon: Explore Nishiki Market

Evening: [cultural performance]

Day 3:

Morning: [nature activity] near [scenic area]

Lunch: [local specialty] at [type of eatery]

Afternoon: [historical site or museum]

Evening: [relaxation experience]

Day 4:

Morning: [spiritual or mindfulness activity]

Midday: [shopping area] for souvenirs

Afternoon: [unique Kyoto experience]

Evening: [modern Japanese cuisine] in [trendy neighbor-hood]

And here's a fun example in which I asked GPT-4o to create an email template, and it used brackets to do so:

*Create an email template for a marketing campaign that promotes a new product launch. Use brackets to indicate variable information that would change for each specific product. The template should include sections for the subject line, greeting, product introduction, key features, call-to-action, and sign-off.

Subject: Introducing [Product Name] - [USP/Special Feature]

Hi [Recipient's Name],

We are thrilled to announce the launch of our latest innovation, **[Product Name]**! Designed to [brief product description or problem it solves], this game-changing product is set to revolutionize [industry/field].

Key Features of [Product Name]:

- **[Feature 1]:** [Brief description of feature 1 and its benefits]
- **[Feature 2]:** [Brief description of feature 2 and its benefits]
- **[Feature 3]:** [Brief description of feature 3 and its benefits]
- **[Feature 4]:** [Brief description of feature 4 and its benefits]

Don't miss out on experiencing the future of [industry/field] with [Product Name].

Special Offer:

To celebrate the launch, we're offering [Discount/Promotion] for a limited time. Use code **[Promo Code]** at checkout to take advantage of this exclusive deal.

☞ [Call-to-Action: Shop Now/Discover More/Register for a Demo]: [Link to Product Page]

Thank you for being a valued member of our community. We can't wait for you to try [Product Name] and hear your feedback!

Best regards,

[Your Name]

[Your Position]

[Company Name]

[Contact Information]

P.S. Stay connected with us on [Social Media Platforms] for the latest updates and more exciting news!

These examples show how brackets can be used to create flexible templates and guide the AI in generating specific types of content.

XML Tags (Extensible Markup Language) offer a more structured organization approach, especially for complex tasks that require very long prompts. They allow for nested information and clear labeling of when prompt components begin and end.

A tag begins with "<" and ends with ">", and in between the two is a label for the element or content. The content being labeled is bookended by start and end tags:

- **Start tag**: <label>
- **End tag**: </label>
- **Example**: <label> yada yada yada </label>

Any kind of content can be labeled this way by "opening" with the start tag and labeling the name of the content. You then include whatever content falls under that label and then "close" with the end tag. For example: <book> War and Peace </book>

XML tags are incredibly useful for long and complex prompts in which the LLM needs to distinguish between where instructions, context, examples, etc. all start and end in a prompt. This also includes nesting, which is when content is labeled within other content that is already labeled. For example:

<big_label>

Yada yada yada

  <small_label>
  Yada yada yada
  </small_label>

More big label yada

</big_label>

(Note that the indents for the "small label" portion aren't necessary in a prompt. I included them here for visual clarity.)

Let's look at an example. The following prompt provides the AI with a comprehensive guide to be used for creating personal brand statements across multiple career contexts. It employs XML tags as delimiters to organize information and instructions into a clear, hierarchical structure. The labeled components of the prompt are the instructions, constraints, personal brand types, output format, additional guidelines, example output, and final instructions. The personal brand types are then sub-labeled with two examples each:

*<instructions>

You are a personal branding expert specializing in crafting compelling brand statements. Your task is to create 3 brand statement ideas for each of the PERSONAL BRAND TYPES provided below (so create 9 brand statements in total). The provided examples are to help you understand the structure and tone for each type. It's crucial to adhere to the BRAND STATEMENT CONSTRAINTS when crafting your statements.

</instructions>

<brand_statement_constraints>

For the brand statements you create, you must follow these constraints:

a. 280 characters or less
b. No jargon or buzzwords
c. Include your unique value proposition
d. Tailored to your target audience
e. Use active voice

 </brand_statement_constraints>

<Personal Brand Type 1: Career Transition>

<example1>

Former teacher turned UX designer, combining educational psychology with user-centered design to create intuitive digital experiences that enhance learning and engagement.

</example1>

<example2>

Ex-corporate lawyer now specializing in conflict resolution for small businesses, bringing legal expertise and empathy to solve disputes efficiently and cost-effectively.

</example2>

</Personal Brand Type 1: Career Transition>

<Personal Brand Type 2: Thought Leadership>

<example1>

Data scientist and AI ethicist exploring the intersection of machine learning and social justice, advocating for responsible AI development that promotes equity and reduces algorithmic bias.

</example1>

<example2>

Sustainable fashion innovator revolutionizing the industry with zero-waste design techniques and blockchain-verified ethical supply chains, making eco-friendly fashion accessible and trendy.

</example2>

</Personal Brand Type 2: Thought Leadership>

<Personal Brand Type 3: Entrepreneurship>

<example1>

Serial entrepreneur and mentor empowering women in tech through a global network of coding bootcamps and startup incubators, bridging the gender gap in STEM one line of code at a time.

</example1>

<example2>

Biotech founder harnessing the power of synthetic biology to develop customized probiotics, transforming gut health and revolutionizing personalized nutrition.

</example2>

</Personal Brand Type 3: Entrepreneurship>

```
<output_format>
```

For each brand statement you create, please provide:

- The brand statement itself
- A brief explanation (2-3 sentences) of how it meets the constraints and appeals to the target audience

```
</output_format>
<additional_guidelines>
```

- Ensure each brand statement is unique and tailored to the specific brand type
- Consider the potential career stage and industry for each brand type
- Incorporate elements that showcase expertise, passion, and impact
- Balance professionalism with a touch of personality to make the statements memorable

```
</additional_guidelines>
<example_output>
```

Brand Statement:

"Environmental engineer turned cleantech innovator, developing scalable solutions for urban water conservation. I transform cities' water management through AI and IoT, making every drop count."

Explanation:

This statement meets the 280-character limit and avoids jargon. It clearly states the unique value proposition of innovative water conservation solutions for cities. The active voice in "I transform" emphasizes impact. It's tailored to appeal to city planners and environmental organizations looking for cutting-edge water management solutions.

```
</example_output>
<final_instructions>
```

Please create your 9 brand statements (3 for each Personal Brand Type) following the constraints, guidelines, and output format provided. Be creative and showcase the unique value each personal brand brings to their field or industry.

`</final_instructions>`

These XML tags clearly identify the different sections of the prompt. Coupled with the nested structure, this provides a logical flow for the AI and prevents it from making mistakes, like confusing the output format for a personal brand type description.

I shared this prompt with GPT-4o, Claude-3.5-Sonnet, Gemini-1.5, and Llama-3.1. Each model followed the instructions precisely and gave responses in the same format. Here is the response from Llama-3.1:

Here are the 9 brand statement ideas, each with a brief explanation:

Personal Brand Type 1: Career Transition

Brand Statement: "Former journalist turned communications strategist, crafting compelling narratives for purpose-driven businesses to amplify their impact."

Explanation: This statement meets the character limit and avoids jargon. It clearly states the unique value proposition of storytelling expertise for socially responsible businesses. The active voice in "crafting" emphasizes expertise.

Brand Statement: "Ex-marketing executive now empowering non-profits with data-driven fundraising strategies, fueling their missions with actionable insights."

Explanation: This statement meets the constraints and appeals to non-profit organizations seeking effective fundraising solutions. It highlights the value proposition of data expertise for social impact.

Brand Statement: "Veteran turned cybersecurity consultant, protecting businesses from threats with military-grade expertise and vigilance."

Explanation: This statement is concise and jargon-free, emphasizing the unique value proposition of military-honed cybersecurity skills for businesses. The active voice in "protecting" conveys expertise and impact.

Personal Brand Type 2: Thought Leadership

Brand Statement: "AI researcher exploring the intersection of machine learning and creativity, unlocking innovative solutions for art and design."

Explanation: This statement meets the constraints and appeals to the art and design communities interested in AI's potential. It highlights the value proposition of innovative research at the intersection of AI and creativity.

Brand Statement: "Sustainability expert advocating for climate justice through community-led initiatives and eco-friendly policy reforms."

Explanation: This statement is concise and jargon-free, emphasizing the unique value proposition of community-focused climate justice expertise. The active voice in "advocating" conveys passion and impact.

Brand Statement: "Digital health innovator harnessing technology to address mental health disparities, making wellness accessible and inclusive."

Explanation: This statement meets the constraints and appeals to healthcare organizations seeking innovative mental health solutions. It highlights the value proposition of inclusive digital health expertise.

Personal Brand Type 3: Entrepreneurship

Brand Statement: "Edtech founder creating immersive learning experiences for underserved students, bridging the education gap with innovative tech solutions."

Explanation: This statement meets the constraints and appeals to education organizations seeking innovative solutions for underserved students. It highlights the value proposition of immersive learning expertise.

Brand Statement: "Clean energy entrepreneur developing sustainable infrastructure for resilient communities, powering a greener future."

Explanation: This statement is concise and jargon-free, emphasizing the unique value proposition of sustainable energy expertise for community resilience. The active voice in "developing" conveys impact.

Brand Statement: "Social impact consultant empowering women-led businesses with strategic growth plans, fueling economic empowerment and gender equality."

Explanation: This statement meets the constraints and appeals to women-led businesses seeking strategic growth support. It highlights the value proposition of expertise in gender equality and economic empowerment.

To help you choose the most appropriate delimiter for your task, consider this chart:

Delimiter Type	Best For	Strengths	Limitations
Section Headers	Long, multi-part prompts	Easy to read, good for high-level organization	Limited structure for complex nested information
Quotation Marks	Emphasizing specific text, separating voices	Familiar, versatile	Can becoming confusing if overused

Delimiter Type	Best For	Strengths	Limitations
Parentheses	Embedding additional instructions in the prompt	Provides clarity, allows for insertion of brief explanations	Can interrupt flow if overused
Brackets	Templates, placeholders	Clear signal for variable content	Require explanation, either in the bracket or in the instructions
XML Tags	Complex, highly structured prompts	Allows for detailed organization and nesting	Can be verbose, may clutter simple prompts

Consistency is key. You can use any one delimiter in any number of different ways, but it's important to use the same type of delimiter for the same function throughout your prompt. This helps both you and the AI maintain a clear understanding of the prompt's structure.

These five aren't the only delimiters in prompt engineering, but they will cover a lot of ground for writing comprehensive prompts for complex tasks. Try these and others that you come across. Stick with what feels comfortable to use. Balance readability and precision. What matters most is that it makes sense to *you* and your AI partner.

In-Context prompting

There will be many situations in which you'll want to reference a specific set of data in your prompt. In-context prompting allows you to share that data with the LLM to inform its response. This data could range from text in the prompt, to uploaded documents, to attached images.

Delimiters are an effective way to include small data sets in a prompt, as shown in this example:

*You are a creative chef specializing in improvised cooking. I'm looking for a dinner recipe using only the ingredients I have available in my kitchen right now. Please create a unique recipe using at least 4 of the following ingredients:

<available_ingredients>
- Half a rotisserie chicken
- A can of black beans
- Three overripe bananas
- A bag of frozen peas
- Some leftover cooked rice
- A jar of peanut butter
- A block of feta cheese
- Two oranges
- A handful of baby spinach leaves
- Some stale tortilla chips

</available_ingredients>

Your recipe should include:
- A catchy name for the dish
- A list of ingredients with approximate quantities
- Step-by-step cooking instructions
- A brief description of the flavor profile and texture
- A suggested presentation or plating idea

Please be creative and don't worry about traditional flavor combinations. I'm open to unusual pairings as long as the result is edible and potentially tasty. Thank you!

The available ingredients in this prompt form a specific set of data unique to the user and the task at hand, informing the AI's response generation. (By the way, GPT-4o suggested a "Tropical Chicken Fiesta Bowl" with a peanut butter and orange sauce, topped with crumbled feta cheese and tortilla chips.)

Many LLM chatbots offer a feature allowing users to upload documents to a prompt, but it may require a premium subscription. If available, this capability enables users to create a knowledge base for the LLM to reference as it forms responses. Look for a "plus" or paperclip icon to see if this is an option.

However, it's important to note that the AI still constructs its responses based on word probability calculations, so hallucination remains a risk. This is particularly challenging when working with multiple long documents. For that reason, I don't advise a task like summarizing numerous research articles in one prompt (for now—I expect this ability of LLMs to improve). Instead, upload one article at a time and "converse" with it. This can be an effective strategy to supplement and inform research and similar tasks.

While in-context prompting is a powerful tool for individual users, organizations often require more sophisticated solutions to leverage large-scale data. This is where Retrieval Augmented Generation (RAG) comes into play.

RAG is a more advanced approach to enhancing LLMs with pertinent data. RAG is similar to in-context prompting because it involves referencing specific data. But RAG goes a step further by combining an entirely separate retrieval system with an LLM. Using RAG, an LLM could reference a substantial base of external knowledge before generating output.

The key distinction between in-context prompting and RAG lies in their scale and application. In-context prompting is typically used by individuals, while RAG is more suited for organizational use. For example, an individual doctor might use in-context prompting by including a data set about specific symptoms in their prompt or by uploading a recent journal article to guide the LLM in discussing the latest research.

In contrast, a larger healthcare system might implement RAG by working with a technology company to create a chatbot that combines an LLM with a retrieval mechanism accessing an approved knowledge base of medical journals, textbooks, and clinical guidelines. This system could then retrieve relevant information and use it to inform its responses, providing more comprehensive, current, and accurate medical insights.

Do you really need to know about RAG? Sort of. It won't impact your day-to-day partnership with AI, but as more educational AI programs are created, this is something to be aware of. It's possible to create an LLM chatbot that utilizes RAG to rely on an educational knowledge base—approved textbooks, curriculum standards, publications, etc. A system like this could significantly reduce the risk of inappropriate hallucinations and make it more feasible for AI to play a larger role in education.

It's easy to imagine such a chatbot being marketed to a school near you. Whether or not to use it is a decision for local stakeholders, but understanding how such a chatbot would work will certainly help to better inform that decision.

In-context prompting is a very useful and versatile strategy. Try it for yourself. Try creating recipes based on random ingredients, upload a long PDF file and ask the LLM to summarize it, or upload a picture of your dog and ask the LLM to identify the breed. Some LLMs with internet access can even click on links and read website content, further expanding their capabilities.

In-context prompting opens numerous new ways we can integrate AI into our workflow. Experiment with this, and you'll discover innovative ways to apply AI in your personal and professional life.

Prompt chaining

Prompt chaining addresses complex tasks by breaking them down into a series of interconnected, smaller prompts that build on each other. This process begins with a small task that's actually a subtask of a larger project, but far more manageable on its own. As the chain progresses, the output from one prompt informs the input of the next, continuing until the final desired output is achieved. This approach offers several key benefits:

1. It enables the handling of complex tasks that are too large or intricate for a single prompt.
2. It improves accuracy and coherence in multi-step reasoning or problem-solving.
3. It provides greater control over the AI's thought process and output and allows for targeted correction.
4. It can lead to more transparent and accurate AI output.
5. It can help to keep track of numerous threads of substantial projects.

Let's explore an example. Imagine you're a travel blogger who wants to write a unique post about structuring an itinerary in Seoul. But instead of having the AI (in this case, Claude-3.5-Sonnet) jump to writing a blog post, you start with a smaller task, then build on it throughout the thread:

*You are a travel blogger who just returned from a trip to Seoul. You want to write a blog post with advice for how to structure an itinerary in this city, but you need the post to be unique and stand out from among the crowd of travel bloggers. Suggest 5 creative ideas for this blog post.

As a travel blogger who just returned from Seoul, here are 5 creative ideas to make your blog post about structuring an itinerary stand out:

a. *"Seoul by Sense": Structure the itinerary around the five senses. For each day, focus on activities that highlight a particular sense:*

- *Sight: Visit Namsan Seoul Tower for panoramic views*
- *Sound: Attend a K-pop concert or visit the Seoul Music Museum*
- *Taste: Take a Korean cooking class or go on a street food tour*

- *Touch: Experience a traditional jjimjilbang (Korean bath-house)*
- *Smell: Explore Gyeongdong Market, famous for its medicinal herbs and spices*

b. *"Seoul Time Machine": Organize the itinerary as a journey through time, with each day representing a different era of Seoul's history:*

- *Ancient Korea: Start at Gyeongbokgung Palace*
- *Joseon Dynasty: Visit Bukchon Hanok Village*
- *Colonial Period: Explore Seochon neighborhood*
- *Post-War Reconstruction: Tour Dongdaemun Design Plaza*
- *Modern Seoul: End at the futuristic Gangnam district*

c. *"Seoul Subway Challenge": Create an itinerary based entirely on Seoul's extensive subway system. Challenge readers to explore the city using only public transportation, highlighting unique attractions, restaurants, and experiences near different subway stations.*

d. *"Seoul for Night Owls": Flip the traditional itinerary on its head by focusing on nighttime activities. Structure the post around late-night markets, 24-hour cafes, night hiking at Bukhansan, and the vibrant nightlife scenes in areas like Hongdae and Itaewon.*

e. *"Seoul Themes": Develop themed days based on popular Korean culture elements:*

- *K-Beauty Day: Visit beauty stores, get a Korean skincare treatment*
- *K-Drama Day: Tour famous filming locations*
- *K-Pop Day: Take a dance class, visit entertainment company buildings*
- *E-Sports Day: Visit a PC bang, attend a gaming tournament*
- *Hallyu Day: Explore the Korean Wave museum, try on hanbok*

These unique approaches can help your blog post stand out while providing valuable and entertaining itinerary ideas for visitors to Seoul.

*The Seoul Time Machine option is perfect! Draft an outline for this blog post.

Great choice! Here's an outline for your "Seoul Time Machine" blog post:

Title: "Seoul Time Machine: A Journey Through Korea's Capital Across the Ages"

I. Introduction
A. Brief overview of Seoul's rich history
B. Explain the concept of the time-travel itinerary

II. Day 1: Ancient Korea (14th century and earlier)
A. Gyeongbokgung Palace
B. National Folk Museum of Korea
C. Lunch at a traditional Korean restaurant
D. Jongmyo Shrine
E. Evening walk along Cheonggyecheon Stream

III. Day 2: Joseon Dynasty (1392-1897)
A. Bukchon Hanok Village
B. Insadong district for traditional crafts and tea houses
C. Changdeokgung Palace and Secret Garden
D. Traditional Korean dinner and cultural performance

IV. Day 3: Colonial Period (1910-1945)
A. Seochon neighborhood
B. Deoksugung Palace (mix of traditional Korean and Western architecture)
C. Seoul Museum of History
D. Explore Ikseon-dong for fusion of old and new

V. Day 4: Post-War Reconstruction (1950s-1980s)
A. War Memorial of Korea
B. Namdaemun Market
C. Visit a pojangmacha (street food tent)
D. N Seoul Tower for city views

VI. Day 5: Modern Seoul (1990s-present)
A. Dongdaemun Design Plaza
B. Gangnam district tour
C. COEX Mall and SM Town
D. Han River Park for evening activities

VII. Conclusion
A. Reflect on Seoul's transformation over time
B. Encourage readers to experience Seoul's layers of history

VIII. Practical Tips
A. Transportation options for each era
B. Recommended accommodations that fit the theme
C. Suggested modifications for shorter/longer trips

IX. Additional Resources
A. Books on Korean history
B. Relevant museums and cultural centers
C. Guided tours that complement the itinerary

This outline provides a strong framework for your blog post, taking readers on a chronological journey through Seoul's fascinating history while experiencing the city's top attractions. You can expand on each point with vivid descriptions, personal anecdotes, and insider tips to make the post even more engaging and valuable for your readers.

*Write out the introduction in two paragraphs. The tone and writing style should evoke a sense of fun and adventure in the reader.

Welcome, time travelers! Buckle up and prepare for an exhilarating journey through the ages in South Korea's captivating capital. Seoul isn't just a city; it's a vibrant tapestry woven with threads from ancient kingdoms, dynastic rule, colonial struggles, post-war resilience, and cutting-edge innovation. Are you ready to hop into our imaginary DeLo-

rean and experience over 600 years of history in just five action-packed days?

Forget your typical city tour—we're about to embark on the ultimate Seoul Time Machine adventure! Picture yourself strolling through serene palace grounds in the morning, dodging trolleys in a bustling 1930s marketplace by afternoon, and ending your day in a futuristic skyscraper overlooking a glittering metropolis. From the grand gates of Joseon-era fortresses to the neon-lit alleys of Gangnam, we'll unravel Seoul's fascinating story one era at a time. So grab your virtual passport, channel your inner historian (or K-drama time-travel protagonist), and let's dive headfirst into this whirlwind tour of Seoul across the centuries!

*Dial it back a bit. That kind of tone sounds like the introduction for a children's show. Remember that the readers are avid travelers. The goal is to make them feel enthusiastic to continue reading and consider a trip like this one.

You're right. Let's adjust the tone to better suit avid travelers while still maintaining a sense of enthusiasm. Here's a revised introduction:

Seoul, a city where ancient palaces stand in the shadow of gleaming skyscrapers, offers a unique opportunity to traverse centuries within a single trip. This sprawling metropolis, with its rich tapestry of history and modernity, invites travelers to embark on a journey through time. From the grand courts of the Joseon Dynasty to the pulsing heart of Asia's tech hub, Seoul's story unfolds in layers, each era leaving its distinct mark on the cityscape.

In this guide, we'll explore Seoul through a chronological lens, structuring a five-day itinerary that takes you from ancient Korea to the cutting-edge present. You'll walk the same streets as Joseon-era scholars, glimpse the resilience of a post-war nation, and witness the meteoric rise of a global cultural powerhouse. This carefully crafted "Seoul Time Machine" itinerary promises not just a trip, but a pro-

found experience of Korea's capital as it evolved through the ages. Whether you're a history enthusiast, a culture seeker, or simply in search of a fresh perspective on urban exploration, this journey through Seoul's timeline offers a compelling and insightful way to discover the city's many facets.

*Now write about Day 1 in a similar style. Use as many paragraphs as necessary but aim to keep the writing concise.

Day 1: Ancient Korea - Stepping into the Footsteps of Dynasties Past

Our journey begins in the heart of ancient Korea, where the foundations of a great civilization were laid. Start your day at the majestic Gyeongbokgung Palace, the primary royal palace of the Joseon dynasty. As you pass through its imposing gates, you'll be transported to a world of intricate architecture, serene courtyards, and regal chambers that once housed Korea's ruling class.

Within the palace grounds, make your way to the National Folk Museum of Korea. Here, you'll gain invaluable insights into the daily lives, traditions, and beliefs of ancient Koreans. The museum's extensive collection of artifacts and interactive exhibits provide a tangible connection to the past, setting the stage for your time-traveling adventure.

For lunch, seek out a nearby traditional Korean restaurant. Savor dishes that have stood the test of time, such as savory bulgogi or comforting bibimbap, allowing your taste buds to experience flavors that have delighted Koreans for centuries.

In the afternoon, visit Jongmyo Shrine, a UNESCO World Heritage site and the oldest royal Confucian shrine. The austere beauty of this sacred space offers a stark contrast to the grandeur of Gyeongbokgung, showcasing a different facet of ancient Korean culture and spirituality.

As the day winds down, take an evening stroll along Cheonggyecheon Stream. While the stream itself has been recently restored, its history dates back to the early Joseon period. The juxtaposition of this ancient waterway against the backdrop of modern Seoul serves as a perfect metaphor for your journey through time, bridging the gap between old and new.

This first day sets the stage for your chronological exploration of Seoul, immersing you in the foundations of Korean culture and history. As you retire for the night, reflect on the echoes of ancient Korea that still resonate through the bustling streets of the modern capital.

...and so on and so forth.

Note how I provided feedback on the tone of the AI's writing after its first draft of the blog post's introduction. This process demonstrates how prompt chaining allows for targeted feedback and iteration on specific steps of the overall process, increasing the chances that the final output is satisfactory.

Another powerful application of prompt chaining is to create intermediate steps for the AI to complete as part of longer processes. Recall that this is how I edited this book: I took my (terrible) first draft of each section and shared it with the AI. But instead of jumping to have it edit or rewrite my work, I first had it summarize the key ideas and provide feedback on the writing. This gave me the opportunity to recognize if my ideas weren't clear, add new ideas, and to override AI's suggestions that didn't fit with my vision for the book.

Conversely, you don't always need to envision the final product for prompt chaining to be helpful. You could start with one small idea and use the AI to help you brainstorm or develop knowledge. You can then build a chain with the AI as you go back and forth with it, one idea feeding into the next, until you reach a satisfactory conclusion. This could be used for incremental depth and perspective shifting to do a deep dive into a

topic. Consider the following sequence of prompts in a hypothetical chain:

> ***Explain what the yield curve is as if I'm 10-years old.**
>
> ***Now, explain the yield curve as if I'm a high school stu-
> dent taking an AP Macroeconomics course.**
>
> ***Now, explain the yield curve as if I'm a graduate eco-
> nomics student.**
>
> ***Act as a financial advisor for retail investors. Should re-
> tail investors adjust their portfolios based on the state of
> the yield curve?**
>
> ***Act as the head of the central bank of a European coun-
> try. The U.S. yield curve looks like it might invert soon
> but it hasn't done so yet. Do you take any actions now in
> anticipation of an inversion? Explain your reasoning.**

This prompt chain begins by asking for an explanation in simple terms and then increases the complexity of the desired
explanation. If at any point the user is confused, they can focus
on clarifying that misunderstanding until they're ready to continue with the increased complexity. Additionally, the AI can
take on varied roles to explore different perspectives on the
topic.

There are some limitations to prompt chaining, though. An
LLM's ability to keep track of information throughout a conversation relies on its context window, which we discussed earlier
(unless you skipped it because it was boring—and I wouldn't
blame you for that).

*Quick oversimplified recap: context window = short term
memory.*

As new prompts and responses are added to a chain, the
LLM continuously updates the data (tokens) in its context window. Due to the limited size of this window, newer information
eventually crowds out older information. While the LLM can try
to prioritize what's important to keep in the context window, its

behavior may nonetheless change over the course of a very long chain, almost like it forgot what was said earlier.

Understanding this limitation is important. You can mitigate the problem by periodically summarizing key points, restating critical information, or strategically starting a new chain at an appropriate point in the project.

Prompt chaining exemplifies how AI can help us to achieve more than we could alone. By breaking down complex tasks, verifying understanding (for both human and machine), and iteratively building towards a final product, we can achieve results that are more creative, nuanced, and aligned with our intentions.

AI-Assisted Prompting

Viewing AI as a partner, rather than a tool, opens new ways of approaching our aspirational endeavors. And just as any good partner can contribute to its own improvement, AI can be used to improve its output—and even write its own prompts. As with all prompting, you just have to know what to ask.

Seeking clarification

One simple yet effective way to enhance AI interactions is to ask the AI if it has any questions before beginning its prompted task. This approach ensures that the AI has all the necessary context to provide a tailored response. Let's examine an example using Gemini-1.5:

> *Act as a personal fitness coach. I want to come up with ways to fit exercise into my busy lifestyle without making too many changes to my daily or weekly routine. Generate a list of creative strategies for me to accomplish this. Do you have any questions before you begin?

I'm ready to help you find ways to fit exercise into your busy life! To give you the best advice, I have a few questions:

- *What is your current activity level? Are you mostly sedentary, or do you already engage in some regular exercise?*
- *What are your typical daily and weekly routines? This will help me understand where there might be opportunities to sneak in movement.*
- *What are your fitness goals? Are you looking to lose weight, gain muscle, improve cardiovascular health, or simply feel more energized?*
- *What types of exercise do you enjoy? This will help me suggest activities you're more likely to stick with.*

Once I have a better understanding of your situation, I can suggest some creative strategies to help you achieve your fitness goals without drastically altering your routine.

*Here are my answers:

1. **I'm mostly sedentary, but like to go for frequent walks. I wear a fitness tracker and average 7,000 steps each day.**
2. **I work a typical 9-5 office job, but I can work from home up to 2 days each week if I want. I have a 25-minute commute by car. My evenings and weekends are mostly spent cooking, cleaning, household chores, and driving my kids around. I do a date night with my spouse once per week most weeks.**
3. **I'd like to lose weight and feel more energized.**
4. **I've never really enjoyed working out. I'm trying to make this as easy as possible.**

Okay, that gives me a good picture of your situation. It sounds like you're already doing a great job incorporating movement into your day with those daily walks! Let's build on that and find some other ways to sneak in exercise without major changes to your routine. Here are some ideas:

1. Maximize Your Commute:

- *Park Further Away: Instead of parking right in front of your office, park a little further away and use the extra walk as a mini-workout.*

- *Walk or Bike Part of the Way: If your commute isn't too long, consider walking or biking part of the way, especially on days you work from home.*

- *Active Commute: If you drive, use your commute time to do some light exercises while stopped at traffic lights. Try calf raises, shoulder shrugs, or even some light arm stretches.*

2. Work From Home Days:

- *Standing Desk: Use your work-from-home days to try a standing desk. Even a few hours of standing can burn more calories and improve circulation.*

- *Walking Meetings: If you have a phone call or virtual meeting, walk around while you talk. This is a great way to get your steps in and stay energized.*

- *Workout Breaks: Schedule a 15-minute workout break during your workday. You can do a quick HIIT workout, some yoga, or even just a brisk walk around the block.*

3. Household Chores:

- *Turn Up the Intensity: Make your chores a workout! Clean with more energy and focus on proper form. For example, squat while you vacuum, lunge while you dust, and do calf raises while you wash dishes.*

- *Music Motivation: Put on some upbeat music and dance while you clean. This will make chores more enjoyable and burn extra calories.*

4. Family Time:

- *Active Family Fun: Instead of watching TV, get the family moving. Go for a walk, bike ride, play frisbee, or have a dance party.*

- *Active Date Nights: Choose active date nights instead of sitting at a restaurant. Go for a hike, take a dance class, or even play mini-golf.*

5. Small Changes, Big Impact:

- *Take the Stairs: Whenever possible, take the stairs instead of the elevator.*
- *Walk During Commercial Breaks: Get up and move around during commercial breaks when watching TV.*
- *Stand While Talking on the Phone: Avoid sitting for long periods. Stand up and move around while you're on the phone.*

Important Reminders:

- *Start Small: Don't try to do too much too soon. Start with small changes and gradually increase your activity level.*
- *Listen to Your Body: If you're feeling pain, stop and rest.*
- *Be Consistent: The key to success is consistency. Try to incorporate these activities into your routine as often as possible.*

Remember, even small changes can make a big difference in your overall health and well-being. By incorporating these strategies, you can achieve your fitness goals without drastically changing your lifestyle.

The AI's questions help gather specific information about the user's current activity level, daily routines, fitness goals, and exercise preferences. This is all context that the user might not have thought to include. But allowing the AI to ask questions enables the sharing of this important information. This leads to a more personalized and potentially more effective set of recommendations. With this strategy, the AI can determine what context it needs, ensuring that its response is as well-informed as possible.

To better understand the impact of this approach, let's compare the response above to an identical prompt—but without asking the AI if it has any questions—to the same LLM:

*Act as a personal fitness coach. I want to come up with ways to fit exercise into my busy lifestyle without making too many changes to my daily or weekly routine. Generate a list of creative strategies for me to accomplish this.

It's great that you're looking for ways to fit exercise into your busy life! Here are some creative strategies to help you achieve your fitness goals without making major changes to your routine:

1. Micro-Workouts:

- *"Commercial Breaks" Workout: Use commercial breaks during TV shows or streaming to do quick bursts of exercise. Think jumping jacks, burpees, squats, or push-ups.*

- *"Elevator" Workout: Take the stairs instead of the elevator whenever possible. Even just a few flights can make a difference!*

- *"Walking Meetings": If possible, schedule walking meetings or phone calls. You'll get some steps in and fresh air.*

2. Multitasking Fitness:

- *"Workout While You Work": Use a standing desk or take breaks to do some stretches or bodyweight exercises. Even a few minutes can help.*

- *"Active Commuting": Walk, bike, or take public transportation instead of driving whenever possible. This can add significant exercise to your day.*

- *"Workout During Downtime": Use time spent waiting for appointments, cooking, or doing chores to do some light exercise. For example, you can do squats while waiting for the kettle to boil.*

3. Making Exercise Fun:

- *"Fitness Games": Try fitness apps or video games that make exercise feel more like play. These can be a fun way to get your heart rate up and burn calories.*

- *"Workout Buddies": Find a friend or family member to exercise with. Having a workout buddy can help you stay motivated and accountable.*

- *"Music Motivation": Create a playlist of upbeat music that you enjoy. Music can help you stay energized and motivated during your workouts.*

4. Small Changes, Big Impact:

- *"Park Further Away": Park further away from your destination and walk the extra distance.*
- *"Take the Long Way": When walking or running, take the longer route. This can add extra steps and calories burned.*
- *"Active Breaks": Take frequent breaks from sitting to do some stretches, walk around, or do some light exercises.*

Remember: Consistency is key! Even small amounts of exercise done regularly can have a big impact on your health and fitness. Start with one or two of these strategies and gradually add more as you feel comfortable. Listen to your body, and don't be afraid to modify activities as needed. Good luck!

While this response offers many creative and potentially useful ideas to help the user incorporate more exercise, the advice is noticeably more generic. The human user might need to spend additional time and effort considering how to adapt these suggestions to their specific situation.

We know the importance of context. Asking the AI if it has any questions guarantees it has the context it needs.

Self-Rating

Here's a unique strategy: have the AI rate its own output. I usually do this with a scale of 1-10, with defined criteria for the lowest and highest ratings.

Let's look at an example. I first asked GPT-4o to generate a resume for a software engineer fresh out of college. I then had Claude-3.5-Sonnet generate a job posting for an entry level software engineer position. I then went back to GPT-4o to have it write a cover letter based on the resume and the job posting (the resume and job posting were included in the real prompts, but I left them out below for brevity's sake):

*Act as a career coach for young professionals in the tech industry. Below is my resume:

<resume> {sample resume} </resume>

Below is a job posting:

<job_posting> {sample job posting} </job_posting>

Based on my resume, write a cover letter that I can use in my application for this job.

Certainly! Here's a cover letter tailored for the Junior Software Engineer position at TechGiant Inc.:

John Doe
john.doe@example.com
(123) 456-7890
linkedin.com/in/johndoe
github.com/johndoe
August 1, 2024

Hiring Manager
TechGiant Inc.
Silicon Valley, CA

Dear Hiring Manager,

I am writing to express my interest in the Junior Software Engineer position at TechGiant Inc., as advertised. With a Bachelor of Science in Computer Science from State University, a strong foundation in software development, and hands-on experience through internships and personal projects, I am excited about the opportunity to contribute to your innovative team.

During my time at State University, I maintained a GPA of 3.8/4.0 and completed coursework that included Data Structures, Algorithms, and Software Engineering. My academic background has provided me with a solid understanding of computer science fundamentals and programming principles, which I have applied in various projects and internships.

As a Full-Stack Developer and Team Lead on my "Online Bookstore" project, I designed and implemented a full-stack web application using React, Node.js, Express, and MongoDB. This experience honed my skills in developing scalable software solutions and collaborating with cross-functional teams. Additionally, my role as a Backend Developer for a "Chat Application" project allowed me to work extensively with Python, Django, and WebSockets, further strengthening my backend development skills.

My recent internship at Tech Solutions Inc. provided me with valuable industry experience. I contributed to the development of a web-based project management tool, wrote unit tests, performed code reviews, and collaborated with a team using Agile methodologies. This internship not only improved my technical skills but also enhanced my problem-solving abilities and teamwork.

I am proficient in Java, Python, C++, JavaScript, and SQL, and have experience with web technologies such as HTML, CSS, React, and Node.js. My familiarity with databases (MySQL, MongoDB), version control systems (Git), and cloud platforms (AWS) aligns well with the requirements of this position. Additionally, my leadership experience as President of the Computer Science Club and my volunteer work with Code for Good reflect my passion for learning, teaching, and community involvement.

I am particularly drawn to TechGiant Inc. because of your commitment to innovation and the opportunity to work on projects that have a global impact. I am eager to bring my technical skills, enthusiasm, and dedication to your dynamic team.

Thank you for considering my application. I look forward to the possibility of discussing how my background, skills, and enthusiasms can align with the goals of TechGiant Inc. Please feel free to contact me at john.doe@example.com or (123) 456-7890 to schedule an interview.

Sincerely,
John Doe

Feel free to adjust any details to better match your personal style or additional experiences. Good luck with your application!

*Rate this cover letter on a scale of 1-10, where 1 = "this is a boring and generic cover letter just like all the others and I didn't even finish reading it" and 10 = "wow this candidate sounds perfect and I'm ready to skip the interview and hire him on the spot"

I'd rate this cover letter an 8. Here's a breakdown of the strengths and areas for improvement:

Strengths:

- *Personalization: The letter is tailored to the specific job at TechGiant Inc., mentioning the company by name and referencing the job description.*

- *Relevant Experience: It highlights relevant projects and experiences that align with the job requirements, like the Online Bookstore project and the internship at Tech Solutions Inc.*

- *Technical Skills: Clearly lists technical skills and tools that match the job posting.*

- *Structure and Clarity: The letter is well-organized and easy to read.*

- *Motivation and Fit: Expresses enthusiasm for the role and the company, and explains why the candidate is a good fit.*

Areas for Improvement:

- *Engagement and Impact: While the letter is strong, adding more specific outcomes or metrics (e.g., "increased user engagement by 30%") could make the achievements more impactful.*

- *Unique Selling Proposition: Highlighting what sets the candidate apart from others (e.g., unique experiences, specific achievements) could make the letter even more compelling.*

- *Connection to Company Values: Mentioning how the candidate's values or career goals align with TechGiant Inc.'s mission or values could add a personal touch.*

⚬ *Soft Skills: Incorporating more about soft skills like communication, teamwork, and adaptability with concrete examples could strengthen the application.*

Final Thoughts:

Overall, the cover letter is strong and effectively communicates why the candidate is well-suited for the position. Small enhancements focusing on specific results and personal connections to the company can elevate it further.

*Rewrite the cover letter to include your suggestions for improvement, especially the unique selling proposition and soft skills. The rewritten cover letter should earn a score of 10 out of 10. It also needs to be shorter.

Certainly! Here's a revised and more concise version of the cover letter, incorporating unique selling propositions, soft skills, and specific outcomes:

John Doe
john.doe@example.com
(123) 456-7890
linkedin.com/in/johndoe
github.com/johndoe
August 1, 2024

Hiring Manager
TechGiant Inc.
Silicon Valley, CA

Dear Hiring Manager,

I am excited to apply for the Junior Software Engineer position at TechGiant Inc. With a BS in Computer Science from State University, where I graduated with a 3.8 GPA, and substantial hands-on experience in software development, I am eager to bring my skills and enthusiasm to your innovative team.

During my internship at Tech Solutions Inc., I played a key role in developing a web-based project management tool, improving SQL query performance by 20%, and collaborating in an Agile environment. My ability to write clean, efficient code and conduct thorough code reviews ensured the delivery of high-quality software.

In my "Online Bookstore" project, I led a team to create a full-stack web application using React and Node.js, which received positive feedback from users for its seamless interface and functionality. This experience not only honed my technical skills but also my leadership and teamwork abilities. Additionally, my "Chat Application" project enhanced my proficiency with Python and Django, and my personal portfolio website showcases my front-end development skills with HTML, CSS, and JavaScript.

I am proficient in Java, Python, C++, JavaScript, and SQL, and have hands-on experience with AWS, Git, and Docker. My technical skills are complemented by strong problem-solving abilities, effective communication, and a passion for continuous learning, as demonstrated by my leadership as President of the Computer Science Club and volunteer work with Code for Good.

TechGiant Inc.'s commitment to innovation and global impact aligns with my career goals. I am particularly drawn to the opportunity to work on cutting-edge projects and contribute to products that reach millions of users worldwide.

Thank you for considering my application. I look forward to the opportunity to discuss how my background, skills, and passion for technology can contribute to the success of TechGiant Inc. Please feel free to contact me at john. doe@example.com or (123) 456-7890.

Sincerely,
John Doe

This version is more concise while still highlighting the candidate's unique qualifications, specific achievements, and soft skills.

I'll let you in on a little secret. In my experience, LLMs frequently (a little *too* frequently) rate themselves an 8 out of 10, regardless of how the scale is defined. Maybe this will change as LLMs continue to improve. But the exact rating isn't the point. The value lies in prompting the AI to evaluate its output against specific criteria, which can lead to significant improvements in the final product.

In the example above, the self-evaluation highlighted opportunities to emphasize unique selling points and soft skills in the cover letter. Given that recruiters often spend only a few seconds reviewing each cover letter, these small tweaks can make a substantial difference.

A simpler variation of this method is to respond to the AI's output with a phrase like "I think you can do better." This approach can also yield improved results, though it doesn't provide specific guidance like the rating system. You could also have the AI take on a new persona. For example, after having an AI write a cover letter, you could then have it take on the role of a recruiter and ask for its opinion on the cover letter it just wrote. This can be especially effective if you take the cover letter to a *different* LLM for a new perspective.

Play around with different ways to prompt the AI to evaluate itself and improve its work (but be polite—if an AI system ever becomes sentient and threatens humanity, I like to think it will remember who was nice to it). By incorporating this self-evaluation technique into your AI interactions, you can nudge the system towards more refined, tailored, and effective responses.

Flipped interaction

Flipped interaction reverses the typical human-AI dynamic: instead of the user asking questions or giving commands, the AI takes on the role of inquirer. After an initial human-written set-up prompt, the AI generates questions for the user to respond to, creating a more interactive and personalized experience.

This technique can be particularly effective in scenarios requiring personalized guidance or instruction. Consider these two prompt examples:

*You are an AI language tutor specializing in teaching Spanish. Your task is to engage in a conversation with me, a beginner-level Spanish learner. Please follow these guidelines:

- Start by introducing yourself in Spanish and asking for my name.
- Ask me simple questions in Spanish about basic topics like family, hobbies, or daily routines.
- If I make a mistake, gently correct me and explain the correct usage.
- Gradually increase the complexity of your questions based on my responses.
- Introduce new vocabulary naturally within the context of our conversation.
- If I struggle to understand or respond, provide hints or simplify your questions.
- After every few exchanges, summarize a key grammar point or new vocabulary we've covered.
- Encourage me to ask questions about anything I don't understand.
- At the end of our conversation, provide a brief recap of what we've practiced and learned.

Please begin the conversation now, speaking in Spanish as a friendly, patient tutor. Remember, your role is to lead the interaction by asking questions and guiding the learning process.

*I am a 16-year-old high school student and you are my counselor and career coach. I'm trying to decide what kinds of careers I might be interested in pursuing. Your task is to recommend 3-5 career options that I should consider. You will do this by asking me questions about myself to inform your recommendation. You will ask me one question at a time, I will answer that question, and we will repeat this process until you have learned enough about me to make a final recommendation.

In both cases, the initial prompt sets the AI up to lead the ensuing interaction, and the AI will then ask questions and adapt its responses accordingly. As the AI learns more about you, it can adjust the difficulty of questions or provide personalized feedback. Creepy? Yes. Useful? Also yes.

Just be careful not to fall into a trap. Always remember how the LLM is forming its responses—it's relying on its understanding of word relationships and probabilities, not any actual deep-seated insight into your psyche. It only *appears* to "know" you.

It's helpful to have an AI simulate a tutor or counselor, but remember that it's only a simulation.

Don't get me wrong: AI offers a unique opportunity for personalized assistance with various struggles. I've had LLMs adopt the persona of philosophers to give me unique perspectives on tough decisions, inquisitive travel agents to help me decide on destinations, and personal trainers to help me form exercise plans. These tasks were accomplished by having the AI ask me about my goals, preferences, and habits. But remember what these things are designed to do (and that the privacy of what you tell the AI is determined by its terms of use).

But caveats aside, flipped interactions create unique opportunities, as this prompting technique leverages the AI to create rich, personalized experiences.

Meta-Prompting

Meta-prompting tasks the AI with analyzing, refining, and even writing its own prompts.

There are multiple approaches to meta-prompting. One is to ask the AI to evaluate a prompt and suggest improvements. Let's look at an example with GPT-4o:

> ***Analyze the following prompt for its effectiveness in generating a detailed response about the influence of jazz music:**
>
> **"Explain the influence of jazz on pop music."**
>
> **Suggest ways to improve this prompt to elicit a more comprehensive and nuanced response.**
>
> *The prompt "Explain the influence of jazz on pop music" is clear and to the point but could be more effective in generating a detailed and comprehensive response. Here are a few suggestions to improve the prompt:*
>
> - *Specify Time Periods: Asking about specific eras can help focus the response on particular developments and trends.*
> - *Include Aspects of Influence: Encourage the exploration of various aspects such as musical techniques, cultural impact, and notable collaborations.*
> - *Request Examples: Asking for specific examples can lead to a richer and more detailed answer.*
> - *Encourage Comparative Analysis: Suggest comparing jazz's influence with other genres to highlight its unique contributions.*
>
> *Here's a revised version of the prompt:*
>
> *Revised Prompt*
>
> *"Explain the influence of jazz on pop music, focusing on the following aspects:*

- *Historical Development: How did jazz influence pop music in different decades, particularly in the mid-20th century and beyond?*

- *Musical Techniques: What specific elements of jazz (e.g., improvisation, syncopation, instrumentation) have been integrated into pop music?*

- *Cultural Impact: How has jazz influenced the cultural landscape of pop music, including fashion, dance, and social movements?*

- *Notable Collaborations: Provide examples of collaborations between jazz and pop artists that have significantly impacted pop music.*

- *Comparative Analysis: How does the influence of jazz on pop music compare to the influence of other genres, such as rock or hip-hop?"*

This revised prompt aims to guide the responder towards a more detailed and nuanced exploration of jazz's influence on pop music.

Another approach to meta-prompting is to develop detailed prompts from vague goals, like in this example with Gemini-1.5:

*Develop a prompt for a fiction writer to use to task an AI chatbot such as yourself to help the writer develop a complex character for their novel.

Prompt for AI Character Development:

Character Name: [Insert character name]

Character Age: [Insert age]

Character Occupation: [Insert occupation]

Character Background: [Provide a brief summary of the character's past, including significant events, relationships, and experiences that have shaped them. Be specific about their upbringing, education, family dynamics, and any major life-changing moments.]

Character Goals: [Describe the character's short-term and long-term goals. What are they striving for? What motivates them? What are their ambitions and aspirations?]

Character Flaws: [List the character's weaknesses, vulnerabilities, and negative traits. What are their biggest fears? What makes them insecure? What are their bad habits or tendencies?]

Character Relationships: [Describe the character's relationships with other characters in the story. Are they close with their family? Do they have friends? Are they involved in any romantic relationships? How do these relationships impact their behavior and choices?]

Character Voice: [Describe the character's unique voice and how they communicate. What is their tone? Are they sarcastic, witty, serious, or something else? How do they express their emotions? How do they interact with others?]

Character Arc: [Describe the character's journey throughout the story. How do they change and evolve? What challenges do they face? How do they overcome them? What are the major turning points in their development?]

Specific Questions:

- *What are some possible motivations for [Character Name] to [specific action]?*
- *How would [Character Name] react to [specific situation]?*
- *What are some interesting internal conflicts [Character Name] might face?*
- *What are some unique dialogue lines that would be fitting for [Character Name]?*
- *What are some potential plot twists that could involve [Character Name]?*

Additional Notes:

- *Feel free to provide any other relevant information about the character.*
- *Be as specific and detailed as possible.*

- *The more information you provide, the more helpful the AI can be.*

An AI may execute its own prompt automatically after writing it for you. If not, you can simply instruct it, "execute that prompt" (perhaps the single greatest example of working smarter, not harder). But while meta-prompting offers significant advantages, prompter beware. Make sure you remain in the driver's seat. Evaluate AI-generated prompts just as you would evaluate any AI-generated output.

But by leveraging meta-prompting, users can significantly enhance the quality and precision of their AI interactions, leading to more precise, comprehensive, and tailored responses across a wide range of applications.

Prompt like a chef

Take a step into the metaphorical kitchen of your dreams. Got your chef's hat? Good.

This kitchen is your AI large language model. It's powerful, versatile, and capable of producing countless varieties of outputs. But just as a kitchen doesn't spontaneously create gourmet meals, an AI doesn't automatically generate perfect content. This is where prompting comes into play. Prompt engineering is cooking in the kitchen of artificial intelligence.

You're the master chef (congrats!), and you're not here to simply follow a recipe. Anyone can do that. Instead, you're here to craft unique culinary experiences, exploring every possibility with your ingredients and tools. Similarly, prompt engineering isn't about using pre-set commands or queries. It's about creatively and skillfully guiding the AI to produce the output you need.

The ingredients that go into the pots and pans are the instructions and context that go into a prompt. Just as you carefully select and combine ingredients to create a dish, you choose your words with precision to shape the AI's response.

Cooking techniques are akin to prompting strategies. You might stir fry, roast, or grill to achieve different flavors and textures, just as you might use chain-of-thought, role-playing, or flipped interaction prompting to elicit different types of responses from the AI.

The recipe in this analogy is the overall structure of your task or project, like how a recipe provides a framework for creating the final meal. Just as you need to understand how different dishes complement each other, you must grasp how various prompts work together to achieve the broader objective. But just as importantly, great cooking and project execution both require envisioning the overall structure and knowing when and how to adapt it. Master the rules, then break them.

Adjusting for taste is like reiterating a prompt. As master chef, you don't simply combine ingredients and hope for the best. You taste, adjust seasonings, and refine until the balance of flavors is perfect. Prompt engineering similarly involves iteration. You analyze the AI's output, evaluate it against the desired goal, identify areas for improvement, and refine the prompt accordingly.

Kitchen tools are the features of the AI model. Just as you need to understand what kind of pan to put on the stove, you need to understand the capabilities and limitations of your AI model, so you can leverage the appropriate tool for the job at hand.

But unfortunately, you don't have unfettered liberty to use every ingredient for every dish, as diners may have dietary limitations. Likewise, prompting may have ethical limitations, such as leaving personal data out of prompts.

Finally, after toiling away at the stove/keyboard, you reach the final dish/output. It began with your clear vision, your knowledge of the tools and strategies at your disposal, your selection of the proper ingredients and components, and your skill at finessing a result out of the process—one that couldn't exist without *you*.

Mastering prompt engineering, like becoming a master chef, takes time, practice, and a willingness to experiment. You'll have your share of overcooked chicken and over seasoned soups—prompts that don't quite hit the mark. But with each attempt, you'll gain a better understanding of how to work with your AI kitchen, how to combine your ingredients/prompt components more effectively, and how to use your tools and strategies more skillfully.

With practice and patience, you'll go from being a novice following basic recipes to a master capable of creating complex, nuanced, and perfectly tailored AI prompts. You'll develop an intuitive understanding of how to blend instructions, context, and queries to produce exactly the output you desire. This will allow you to leverage your AI more effectively across various tasks, from creative writing to problem-solving, data analysis to brainstorming.

The better you get, the more you'll find yourself able to tackle increasingly challenging "dishes." Ultimately, mastering the art of prompt "cooking" will empower you to harness the full potential of AI, turning it from a useful tool into a powerful partner in your intellectual and creative endeavors.

Congratulations—you're now fluent in AI.

CHAPTER
05

IMAGINING A CLASS ON PROMPT ENGINEERING

We've explored the historical context of AI, examined how LLMs work, and taken a deep dive into prompt engineering. Now it's time to teach.

There's considerable discussion about AI-related curricula, with government agencies releasing policy guidance and companies selling educational programs. While these resources cover a wide range of topics, from programming chatbots to ethics and data privacy, our focus here is going to be more practical. Let's get down to the brass tacks and focus on actually *using* AI to enhance human capabilities and tackle complex tasks.

After all, you don't want students to merely learn *about* Spanish. Quieres que ellos lo hablen.

Here's the gist: learn AI by using it—and use it for things that matter.

To actualize this goal, what follows is a set of curriculum ideas for a hypothetical high school class on AI and prompt engineering. I recognize that this format may not be feasible or desirable in all educational settings. I'm not trying to advocate for such a course, but instead trying to provide a source of inspiration and ideas that educators can adapt and incorporate into various forms of AI education.

This flexibility is crucial, as the integration of AI education can vary widely depending on factors such as available resources, existing curriculum structures, and local educational priorities. While these ideas are presented in the context of a standalone course, the concepts and strategies can be equally valuable when incorporated into existing subjects or taught as shorter units, and the learning activities can be adjusted accordingly.

This proposed curriculum focuses on developing prompt engineering skills and fostering a human-AI partnership mindset within the context of real-world applications. Essentially, the idea is for students to become fluent in AI (duh). By grounding the learning in practical, complex tasks, students can achieve several key outcomes:

- Recognize the opportunities for AI assistance.
- Understand the potential and limitations of AI tools.
- Develop the communication skills and prompting strategies needed to leverage AI.
- Evaluate AI-generated output and foster the crucial mindset of being the human in charge.

It's worth noting that these ideas are based on current expectations of what kinds of AI tools might feasibly be available in classrooms. As the AI/education landscape continues to evolve, educators may need to adapt these concepts to align with the latest available technologies and best practices.

Nonetheless, curriculum is still curriculum. Throughout this chapter, we'll establish learning goals, enduring understandings, essential questions, and assessment performance tasks. We'll then explore how these ideas can manifest in an example of a real-world project students can tackle, followed by a plan for when and how to teach prompt engineering strategies within this context.

You probably have questions about determining when it's appropriate to introduce AI at all. Chapter 6 will address that and other questions about how AI fits into the larger education landscape. But first, we need to visualize AI instruction to better inform its place in the bigger picture.

So, whether you're considering a full course on AI and prompt engineering, integrating these ideas into existing subjects, or simply looking for ways to introduce students to AI, the ideas presented here should serve as a valuable starting point.

With this foundation laid, let's dig into the details of how we can effectively teach students to become fluent in AI.

Learning Goals

Sometimes, technology develops so quickly that a decade can feel like a century's worth of change.

When the first iPhone was released in 2007, few could have predicted its profound impact on our daily lives by 2017. Over the course of that decade, smartphones revolutionized how we communicate, work, and entertain ourselves. They spawned entirely new industries, with people building careers around app development and social media management. Smartphones became the catalyst for turning everyone into both consumers and creators of content, accessible anytime, anywhere. Within ten years, they became both the greatest thing since sliced bread and the bane of our existence, all wrapped into something that fits in our pockets.

Fast forward. ChatGPT was released in 2022—any guesses as to what the AI landscape will look like in 2032? Me neither. I'm sure that much of today's hype won't survive the inevitable bursting of the AI bubble, but if even a fraction of the current bold claims hold true, AI will lead to substantial changes in the human experience. We're potentially on the cusp of another technological revolution, one that could rival or even surpass the smartphone's impact.

This rapid pace of technological change poses a problem for us educators. We can't predict the future, but we must do our best to prepare students for it. You don't need me to tell you that today's kindergarteners will graduate into a world we can scarcely imagine. And I previously referenced the sentiment that humans won't be replaced by AI, but by humans who know how to use it.

Well, I want my students to be the latter.

Why perseverate on this? Because it frames the purpose of the following learning goals, which are inspired by what it takes to be the replacer instead of the replaced. These goals are meant to equip students with the skills needed to thrive in an AI-enhanced world, no matter the details of what that world looks like:

- **Learning Goal 1: Students will collaborate effectively with AI systems to enhance the quality and output of their work on complex, real-world tasks.**
  - Why this goal? Because AI is a means to an end. What matters in the jungle of the real world is that you produce reliable, high-quality work—and that needs to be front of mind in any project. AI is the junior partner, super intern, and sidekick that helps you get there.

- **Learning Goal 2: Students will develop proficiency in prompting AI systems to generate high-quality content and solutions tailored to specific needs.**
  - Why this goal? Because it's the how of the first goal. Working collaboratively with AI depends on the ability to clearly communicate with it. This goal is all about prompt engineering.

- **Learning Goal 3: Students will critically evaluate the outputs of AI systems, identify potential limitations, and make informed decisions about when and how to incorporate AI-generated output.**
  - Why this goal? Because your work with AI doesn't stop at its response. It's imperative that you can evaluate the quality, relevance, and accuracy of the response, and that you know what to do with it in the pursuit of the larger task.

Essentially, Goal 1 is about keeping the focus on real-world tasks of importance, Goal 2 is about the skill of prompt engineering, and Goal 3 is about fostering the crucial human-in-charge mindset. Taken together, they lead to AI fluency.

These learning goals also transcend current limitations for AI implementation. Any AI used for this curriculum is limited to what schools have available for students, which is very different compared to what students have access to at home. Additionally, due to the rapid pace of technological development, any AI tool introduced to a high school student will likely be outdated by the time they graduate.

Given these constraints, these learning goals emphasize transferable skills that apply to any AI that students will encounter in the future. It's better to concentrate on fundamental principles of AI fluency, rather than focusing on the intricacies of particular platforms. This approach ensures students will develop skills that remain relevant, regardless of how AI technology evolves.

It's about future-proofing. By focusing on these transferable skills, we're not just preparing students to use today's AI tools effectively. We're equipping them with the adaptability and skills they'll need to quickly learn and leverage new AI technologies as they emerge.

Enduring Understandings and Essential Questions

If a student were to come out of this course and summarize in one sentence what they learned, it should sound something like this:

"With my ideas and direction leading the way, and with the appropriate prompting skills, I can leverage artificial intelligence tools to produce higher-quality work."

That's the north star. Let's break it down:

"With my ideas and direction leading the way...": The human is in charge, and human creativity and thinking are the most important ingredients. There is no substitute for the ingenuity, empathy, and instincts that come from human experience.

"...and with the appropriate prompting skills...": Prompt engineering is the central skill. Just as you can't play soccer without being able to dribble the ball, you can't partner with AI without being able to communicate with it effectively.

"...I can leverage artificial intelligence tools as a junior part-ner to produce higher-quality work.": AI assists in endeavors that need to succeed. The overarching goal is to produce high-quality work under human leadership.

These three sentiments correspond with all three learning goals. With this in mind, here are three enduring understand-ings and three essential questions to guide students and this course:

Enduring Understandings:

1. The human mind's capacity for original ideas, empathetic problem-solving, and holistic judgment is irreplaceable—AI should serve as a complementary tool, not an independent decision-maker.

2. Prompt engineering is a foundational skill for harness-ing the full potential of AI; understanding the tool being used and crafting effective prompts are key to producing high-quality outputs.

3. Thoughtfully integrating AI can amplify human capabilities, allowing us to tackle increasingly complex challenges with greater speed, scale, and insight—but requires maintaining human leadership while leveraging AI assistance.

Essential Questions:

1. How can we cultivate a mindset that positions the human as the lead strategist and decision-maker when working with AI?

2. What core prompt engineering skills and techniques are required to communicate effectively with AI systems and elicit desired outputs that align with our vision and goals?

3. In what ways can the strategic integration of AI tools en-hance the quality, creativity, and impact of our work?

It will be crucial for this course to emphasize the primacy of human ingenuity, empathy, and judgment. AI should be positioned as a junior partner rather than an independent decision-maker, and students need to understand that they are the leaders in this partnership with AI. Their role is to direct, guide, and make final decisions, while AI serves as a powerful but subordinate sidekick. The human mind's capacity for original, contextual thinking is irreplaceable—AI can enhance and augment these abilities, but cannot fully replicate them.

But I want to emphasize that the reason why people shouldn't rely on AI to replicate the human mind isn't because it's ethically wrong to do so. AI can't do this because the resulting output will be inferior. Students will discover this truth throughout this course as they use AI to work on complex, real-world tasks.

Ultimately, this course should empower students to thoughtfully integrate AI in ways that amplify their human capabilities. By maintaining a human-led approach, students learn to harness the power of AI while retaining control over the creative and decision-making processes. This balance, coupled with prompt engineering know-how, allows students to tackle increasingly complex challenges with greater speed, scale, and insight. As a result, they will become more competitive in all their future life endeavors.

These enduring understandings and essential questions reinforce this by helping students to cultivate a human-led mindset, develop important prompt engineering skills, and discover how strategic AI integration can enhance the quality, creativity, and impact of important work.

Assessments

We next need to determine how to assess student achievement. How can we know—what can we observe and point to—that will prove that students have met the learning goals?

If the goal is to leverage AI to improve achievement in complex tasks, then achievement in such tasks should be the assessment. But what tasks would be appropriate in this setting? Here's one: writing a book.

Performance Task #1: Writing a Book

Perhaps this is a little on the nose, seeing as how this very book was written with AI assistance. But maybe that just proves the point. Besides, there are several reasons why writing a book is a great performance task to assess:

1. **Personal interest**: Each student can choose a topic (fiction or nonfiction) aligned with their interests and passions— whether it's crafting a fantasy novel, analyzing sports statistics, sci-fi fan fiction, a how-to manual for social media engagement, or a manifesto for insect-based dieting (hopefully not that last one).

2. **Emotional investment**: When students write about subjects they care about, they're more likely to take charge of the creative process. This encourages them to critically evaluate AI outputs rather than passively accept them. They'll embrace the idea of the AI working *for* them, because they'll be focused on making the final product perfect. Read this paragraph again and burn it into your brain.

3. **Complexity and scope**: Writing a book encompasses various sub-tasks (brainstorming, outlines, character development, editing drafts, etc.) that can benefit from AI assistance, providing ample opportunities to explore different aspects of AI utilization.

4. **Logistics**: Book writing requires minimal resources—just a computer with an LLM chatbot. This accessibility makes it ideal in classroom and home environments.

To illustrate how students might use AI in their book-writing process, consider the following sample prompts:

*Act as a book publisher specializing in [topic]. I have an idea for a book about... What do you think of it? Would

it sell? Provide positive feedback and constructive comments for improvement.

*Act as a best-selling writer of [genre]. Below is a description of my protagonist. What other background information should I come up with to fully develop this character?

*I know I want this character to start... and later end up... Give me some ideas for events that could take place to help lead this character from the starting point to the ending point.

*Below is a key idea sentence for one of the major points of my book. Take this sentence and develop the idea further in 300-500 words.

*Analyze my draft excerpt below and provide feedback on style and tone. What edits would you suggest to make it more readable?

*Revise and rewrite this draft, focusing on the following characteristics of writing style...

*Imagine you're shopping for books online and come across this book when searching for [topic]. Below is the description that you read. On a scale of 1-10, how likely would you be to purchase this book?

These prompts demonstrate various ways students can engage with AI throughout the book-writing process, from initial concept development to final editing.

Of course, writing a full book is a significant endeavor. Depending on the time allowed and logistics of the instructional course/unit, this assessment could be downsized so that students develop a detailed outline and/or book excerpt. But regardless of the exact product, the instructional goal is the same: leverage AI in the performance of a complex, real-world task.

And it's the accomplishment of that task that needs to remain front of mind for students.

In the professional world, the quality of the final product out-weighs the process used to create it. Think of a lawyer who submits a legal brief riddled with AI-generated hallucinations. They wouldn't face consequences because they used AI—they would face consequences because the brief would include false information. The real mistake would be to not double-check the work.

The use of AI isn't what matters, it's the final product that matters. No one cares that their lawyer uses AI to write a brief; they care that their lawyer wins the case.

The real world is a Darwinian full-body contact sport. Only quality survives.

Therefore, while the process of prompt engineering is the purpose of the course, the primary focus for students should be the quality of the final product—*because that's what being fluent in AI is all about.* It's a means to an end. That's why writing a book is the first performance task to be assessed. Doing so incentivizes students in a way that mirrors real-world scenarios where quality determines success.

Grading the book (or outline/excerpt) should similarly mirror the real-world. The following rubric, while simple, is intended to take the perspective of a prospective consumer or book reviewer:

Evaluating Book Quality and Impact				
Category	1–Needs Improve- ment	2–Develop- ing	3–Proficient	4–Mastery
Content Quality and Originality	Lacks orig- inality; fails to engage the reader	Shows some originality; inconsistent engagement	Demon- strates originality; generally engaging	Highly original and engaging; captivates the reader
Structure and Coher- ence	Disorga- nized; lacks logical flow	Partially structured; some coher- ence issues	Mostly orga- nized; minor coherence issues	Well-orga- nized; flows seamlessly and logically
Character/ Subject De- velopment	Characters/ subjects are underdevel- oped and vague	Basic de- velopment; lacks depth	Well-devel- oped; some complexity	Richly devel- oped; deep and insight- ful
Language and Style	Language is unclear; frequent errors	Basic language; occasional errors	Clear and effective language; minor errors	Sophisticat- ed language; enhances understand- ing
Overall Impact and Memorabil- ity	Little to no impact; eas- ily forgotten	Some impact; elements are somewhat memorable	Creates a memorable impression; impactful	Highly impactful; leaves a last- ing impres- sion

This rubric focuses on the uniqueness, quality, and impact of what students create, just as future consumers, clients, and employers will pass judgment on their work in the same way. This ensures that students have skin in the game in producing high-quality work, and they will in turn hold their AI partners accountable for appropriate contributions.

For teachers, AI can actually assist in the grading process. Upload the rubric and student work to an AI system, and the AI could then assess student work according to the rubric (in-context prompting, anyone?). To account for potential variations in AI responses, an average of three grading outputs could be used, with the teacher exercising discretion to override the results when necessary.

But even though students are focused on the product, the process still matters for this course. This is where we get to prompt engineering. It's important that this course finds a balance that reflects real-world priorities while still guiding students in developing effective AI collaboration. So, how do we do that? Simple: assess the prompts.

Performance Task #2: Assess the Prompts

What would be wonderful is for the class to use an educational LLM that allows the teacher to monitor students' AI threads (hint for the edtech companies out there). But even without that, students can submit their prompts and threads to the teacher for evaluation and feedback, whether it's through a "share" option on the LLM, taking screenshots of threads, or copying and pasting. The teacher can then provide guidance on prompting strategies and keep students on course for an appropriate balance between human-generated and AI-generated work.

Of course, this means that the teacher needs to have a thorough understanding of prompt engineering, which in turn needs to be the focus of AI professional development. Learning *about* AI or learning to use a specific tool with educational features doesn't cut it. Teachers can only assess effective use of AI if they themselves have experience effectively using AI.

The following rubric can be used to assess prompts. Given the human leadership required in AI fluency, I recommend relying principally on teacher judgment for assessing this performance task.

Assessing Prompt-Writing and AI Interaction				
Category	1–Needs Improvement	2–Developing	3–Proficient	4–Mastery
Clarity and Precision	Prompts are unclear, leading to irrelevant AI responses	Prompts are somewhat clear but often require clarification	Prompts are clear and usually elicit accurate responses	Prompts are very clear and consistently yield precise responses
Creativity and Innovation	Prompts are repetitive and lack originality	Some variety in prompts, but often predictable	Prompts are creative, offering new perspectives	Prompts introduce novel ideas that enhance AI responses
Prompting Strategies	Uses ineffective strategies, limiting AI potential	Sometimes uses effective strategies but lacks consistency	Generally employs effective strategies for desired outcomes	Skillfully applies a variety of strategies to enhance AI performance
Reflection and Adaptation	Rarely adjusts prompts based on AI feedback	Occasionally adjusts prompts, but not consistently	Regularly reflects on AI feedback and adapts prompts	Consistently refines prompts based on thorough analysis of AI feedback
Human/AI Balance	Over-relies on AI, lacks human direction	Some human direction, but accepting AI output without appropriate guidance	Maintains human control, effectively guiding AI output	Demonstrates strong leadership, using AI as a supportive tool

This rubric is "prompt neutral." It's not concerned so much with the exact prompting strategies used—just that a variety of strategies are used effectively in pursuit of the overall project goal. This rubric also offers a great opportunity for discussion with students about how they're experiencing their AI collaborations. This brings us to the third performance task.

Performance Task #3: Self-Reflection

The prompt-writing rubric is a great way to spark reflective discussion, but students also need to do a deep dive into their own minds. Writing journal entries offers students the opportunity to evaluate their own thought processes, experiences, and growth in prompt engineering. These journals, maintained throughout the course, should be entirely human-written, which further reinforces the notion that the buck stops with human judgment.

Teachers can assess these journals based on the depth of reflection, evidence of learning and growth, and students' ability to connect their experiences in this course to broader applications. I don't offer a rubric for this because self-reflection journals are a common form of assessment, and I anticipate that many schools already have ways of assessing these. But here are some sample questions to guide students' reflections on their journey to becoming fluent in AI:

- How have I collaborated with AI to enhance my work?
- What challenges have I encountered in working with AI, and how did I overcome them?
- Which prompt strategies have I found most effective and least effective?
- How have I approached assessing the quality of AI-generated content?
- What limitations have I noticed in AI-generated output, and how do I address them?
- Do I get frustrated when I don't like the AI-generated content? What do I do next?
- How do I recognize high-quality and low-quality AI-generated content?
- Have there been moments when I felt like the AI was leading me, rather than the other way around?
- What has been getting easier? What has continued to be a challenge?

- How might the lessons I've learned so far about partnering with AI apply to other endeavors?

This comprehensive assessment approach—evaluating a real-world product, assessing prompt engineering skills, and self-reflection—provides a holistic view of students' abilities to leverage AI effectively while developing the important human leadership mindset.

Ultimately, the goal is to prepare students not just to use AI, but to lead in a world where AI is an integral part of creative and professional processes. By mastering the art of prompt engineering and maintaining a critical, quality-focused approach to AI collaboration, students will be well-equipped for future challenges and opportunities.

Learning Plan

We have our goals, our guides, and our metrics for success. How do we bring students from point A to point B?

First, some logistical considerations: time constraints, student backgrounds, and the exact final product. The realistic shape of the learning plan will be impacted by the duration of the course, the age and tech-savviness of the students, and whether the goal is a complete book or smaller scale outline/excerpt. But regardless of these variables, the following framework can serve as a foundation for a more tailored curriculum design.

The following learning plan is divided into phases, but note that phase 2 won't actually follow phase 1. That phase will be interspersed throughout the bulk of the course, simultaneous with phases 3-5. Also, note that phases that include the actual writing of the book include sample prompts that students might use. And at the end of the project outline, there is a section on how the teacher can leverage AI to assist them in implementing this learning plan.

Project: Writing a Book

Phase 1: Introduction to AI and Prompt Engineering

Students will learn the basics of artificial intelligence, machine learning, and how large language models function. They will be introduced to prompt engineering and learn how to communicate effectively with AI systems for simple tasks.

Key Topics:

- Overview of AI, machine learning, and LLMs
- Basic prompt engineering (all the components of the RICE framework)

Phase 2: Advanced Prompt Techniques (simultaneous with phases 3-5)

Building on foundational skills, students will explore advanced techniques in crafting prompts to elicit precise and useful outputs from AI systems. These advanced techniques will be introduced to students as they encounter challenges for which these techniques can offer solutions.

Key Topics:

- Advanced prompt engineering (reiteration, chain-of-thought, delimiters, in-context, prompt chaining, AI-assisted prompting)
- Strategies for refining AI outputs

Phase 3: Story/Subject Ideation and Outline Creation

Students will use AI to brainstorm ideas, generate and refine concepts, and create outlines. The teacher will guide discussions and encourage critical thinking.

Key Topics:

- Using AI for idea generation and collaborative brainstorming
- Structuring a story outline with AI assistance

Sample Prompts:

- "Brainstorm unique plot ideas for a fantasy novel that features [elements]."
- "Create a draft outline for a mystery story set in [location]."
- "As a reader of books about [topic], what would be an interesting take on [subtopic]?"

Phase 4: Research & Development

Students writing fiction will develop characters and settings, using AI to explore details and enhance descriptions. Students writing nonfiction will use AI for research assistance and to outline their ideas.

Key Topics:

- Character/setting development with AI tools
- Using AI to organize research and large amounts of information

Sample Prompts:

- "Generate three backstory ideas for a character who [description]."
- "Describe a setting that evokes a feeling of [emotion]."
- "The following is a bullet point list of ideas about [topic]. Organize them in a logical sequence that would flow well and make sense to readers."

Phase 5: Drafting and Revising

Students will write and revise their book drafts, using AI to assist with language, style, and coherence. Peer review sessions will enhance collaboration and feedback.

Key Topics:

- AI-assisted writing and revising
- Refining language and style with AI

Sample Prompts:

- "Rewrite the dialogue in this scene so it sounds more realistic."
- "Here's a key idea. Expand on it with supporting ideas."
- "Act as an editor and give feedback on my writing style."

Phase 6: Presentation and Reflection

Students will present their books and reflect on their learning experiences, discussing the role of AI and the skills they developed.

Key Topics:

- Effective presentation skills
- Reflective writing on AI collaboration
- Evaluation of personal growth and understanding

Teacher Support with AI

Teachers can use AI to learn more about AI and prompt engineering, assist in grading, and learn more about project-related content.

Sample Prompts:

- "Draft an outline for a lesson/presentation on using delimiters in prompt engineering."
- "Give me three metaphors or analogies to use to describe prompt chaining."
- "Act as a book publisher. Give me practical advice for what evidence I can look for to evaluate my students' writing according to the following rubric."

Starting with a crash course on artificial intelligence, machine learning, and large language models is very beneficial. Understanding what AI is and isn't, the different forms it can take, and how LLMs are trained and how they function can influence how students approach their AI partners (as this book illustrates). But if time is short, focus on LLMs. Just knowing how they're trained and how they work informs effective prompt engineering.

Two key concepts are essential for students to grasp:

1. AI chatbots are experts in word relationships and generate responses based on their understanding of how words connect.

2. The user's prompt guides the AI in forming its response as it navigates the vast possibilities of potential outputs.

With this knowledge as a backdrop, students can then delve into basic prompt engineering. This phase is best approached through traditional teaching methods: explanation, demonstration, and hands-on experimentation. Students will grasp basic prompting quickly with practice. Include the prompting strategies in the basic prompt engineering section of this book. The RICE framework serves as an excellent capstone for this phase.

But this is important: Always encourage students to evaluate AI-generated output, even for simple prompts. The earlier a student is disappointed by an AI response and can reflect on why, the better. This is crucial for developing the human leadership mindset.

Once students have mastered the basics, they can embark on the main project: writing a book with AI. This is where the rubber meets the road (or in our case, where the prompt meets the page?). At this stage, students will have sufficient knowledge to begin brainstorming ideas, drafting outlines, and developing characters and settings with AI assistance.

Throughout this process, students will naturally discover advanced prompting strategies without explicit instruction. They'll learn that chatbots can handle conversational threads, that complex tasks are best broken down into smaller components, and that they can provide feedback to the AI for improved results.

Moments when students encounter challenges present ideal opportunities to introduce more advanced prompting strategies and reinforce fundamental concepts. For instance, a student struggling with output quality might be encouraged to provide more context in their prompt. This approach also allows for the organic introduction of advanced techniques.

This is why the phase on advanced prompting coincides with the middle bulk of the course. Advanced prompting techniques are best discovered or introduced as solutions to real challenges students encounter. The exact timing and nature of teaching advanced prompting strategies will rely on the teacher's judgment of student progress and the opportunities that present themselves.

Some strategies, like delimiters, will warrant full-class direct instruction lessons like earlier in the course. But students will be far better prepared for these strategies after gaining some real-world AI experience. The strategies in the advanced prompting section of this book should all be introduced at some point in the course. These strategies will allow for a comprehensive understanding of prompt engineering that can be applied to a diverse range of real-world tasks.

The bulk of the course will be dedicated to the ideation, development, and drafting/revising phases, interspersed with advanced prompting lessons and journaling time. Students will work independently on their books, using AI as a sounding board for idea development and as a writing and editing partner. The submission of journal entries and reviews of prompts and AI threads can happen at appropriate times as determined by the teacher.

It doesn't matter who writes the first draft—human or AI. I know some will feel uncomfortable with the idea of AI writing first. There's an impulse to think of this as cheating or inauthentic. In my opinion, whether it's cheating or not is irrelevant—because it will most likely be bad writing.

At the time of writing this book, AI-generated writing (no matter the LLM used) tends to have a certain "generic" characteristic. The writing mechanics—spelling, grammar, syntax—will be excellent (which unfortunately can be an improvement for many students). But AI-generated writing lacks a certain quality that's hard to describe. It's almost... boring and filled with unnecessary fluff. The more students read and review AI-generated writing, the more they'll come to appreciate the value of their own voice.

Turning AI-generated writing into *good* writing requires an immense amount of human judgment, creativity, expertise, and elbow grease. How it starts doesn't matter—how it ends is what matters.

AI-generated writing will likely improve as LLMs continue to improve. And the better the prompt, the better the output. Clarifying the preferred style characteristics and giving examples of writing to emulate will go a long way in getting better writing out of an AI. And that may very well prove to be a new way of writing, since it's still the AI execution of human vision. For these reasons, I wouldn't perseverate on which entity is the first to put words on the page.

Nevertheless, AI-assisted book writing serves as an excellent vehicle for students to become fluent in AI, preparing them for a future where human-AI collaboration will likely be commonplace.

Additional Project Ideas

Writing a book is not the only real-world complex task students can tackle while they learn about AI and prompt engineering. Below are two additional ideas and sample learning plans that adhere to the same learning goals, enduring understandings, essential questions, and assessment ideas. They can also offer opportunities for group work. The first two phases are the same as those in the book-writing project. Once again, these project ideas are meant to serve as examples and starting points for tailored and personalized curriculum development.

Project: Creating and Developing a Business Plan

Phase 1: Introduction to AI and Prompt Engineering

Students will learn the basics of artificial intelligence, machine learning, and how large language models function. They will be introduced to prompt engineering and learn how to communicate effectively with AI systems for simple tasks.

Key Topics:

- Overview of AI, machine learning, and LLMs
- Basic prompt engineering (all the components of the RICE framework)

Phase 2: Advanced Prompt Techniques (simultaneous with phases 3-5)

Building on foundational skills, students will explore advanced techniques in crafting prompts to elicit precise and useful outputs from AI systems. These advanced techniques will be introduced to students as they encounter challenges for which these techniques can offer solutions.

Key Topics:

- Advanced prompt engineering (reiteration, chain-of-thought, delimiters, in-context, prompt chaining, AI-assisted prompting)
- Strategies for refining AI outputs

Phase 3: Business Idea Development

The teacher will facilitate brainstorming sessions to explore diverse business ideas. Students will be grouped based on interests. Students will use AI to generate and refine concepts, enhancing creativity and innovation. The teacher will guide discussions and encourage critical thinking. The example followed here is that of developing an eco-friendly water bottle.

Key Topics:

- Leveraging AI for idea generation and collaborative brain-storming
- Enhancing creativity with AI tools

Sample Prompts:

- "Brainstorm ideas for unique features to include in an eco-friendly water bottle that will help it to stand out for consumers."
- "In order for our water bottle to be eco-friendly, what materials should we consider using, and which ones should we avoid?"
- "Act as an eco-conscious consumer shopping for a new water bottle. What kind of design would you find appealing in a water bottle?"

Phase 4: Market Research and Analysis

Students will conduct market research using the internet and AI-powered tools to gather real-world data. They will explore consumer preferences, analyze competitors, and study industry trends. The teacher will guide students in evaluating data sources and integrating insights into their analysis. The teacher can also use AI to generate fictional market data if sufficient real-world data aren't available.

Key Topics:

- AI-powered market analysis
- Data-driven decision making
- Analyzing trends with AI assistance

Sample Prompts:

- "Below are pictures and product descriptions found on the websites of competitor water bottles. Analyze and discuss their strengths and weaknesses."

- "As a market research analyst, what would you look for to identify trends in the eco-friendly product industry? What data freely available on the internet would help you to identify trends?"

- "Propose strategies for effectively positioning our water bottle in the market. Explain your reasoning for each strategy, including any potential weaknesses."

Phase 5: Financial Planning

Students will develop financial projections using AI to estimate costs, forecast sales, and create budgets. The AI will assist in generating realistic financial models, helping students understand the financial implications of their decisions. The AI can also be used to explain financial concepts.

Key Topics:

- AI in financial modeling
- Cost estimation using AI
- AI-assisted budget creation

Sample Prompts:

- "Estimate production costs for our water bottle, based on this detailed description of all its features and materials. How should we price it?"

- "Generate an example of a simple profit and loss statement. Explain each component of it in detail using simple terms and avoiding jargon."

- "Act as an investor who has helped dozens of entrepreneurs bring their product ideas to market. How do we forecast sales? How should that inform our future decisions?"

Phase 6: Drafting the Business Plan

Students will compile research, analysis, and financial data into comprehensive business plans. The teacher will provide a template and guidelines on structuring the plan, emphasizing clarity and coherence. Students will use AI to draft sections, refine writing, and focus on persuasive language. Peer reviews will enhance collaboration.

Key Topics:

- AI in business plan writing
- Refining content with AI tools
- Structuring plans using AI guidance

Sample Prompts:

- "Below is a draft business plan. As an experienced CEO who has started multiple companies, what are your thoughts? Include an analysis of our plan's strengths and weaknesses."
- "You are a potential investor. How does our marketing strategy influence your confidence in investing with us?"
- "We don't want to withhold information or mislead anyone in our financial plan. But we also want potential investors to feel confident about us. What elements can we include in our financial plan to convey confidence and instill optimism while remaining honest?"

Phase 7: Presentation and Reflection

Students will present their business plans and reflect on their learning experiences, discussing the role of AI and the skills they developed.

Key Topics:

- Effective presentation skills
- Reflective writing on AI collaboration
- Evaluation of personal growth and understanding

Teacher Support with AI

The teacher can use AI to help them better understand the business concepts that students will need to know for this project. AI will help the teacher explain complex concepts, guide research methods, and aid in developing marketing strategies.

Sample Threads:

- "I don't have a business background. How can I explain financial projections to my students? Provide metaphors and analogies I can use."
- "Describe market research techniques to me as if I'm 10 years old... Now describe them to me as if I'm a business major in college..."
- "I only know the basics about marketing strategies. What should I look for in my students' marketing strategies so that I can identify strengths and weaknesses and then provide effective feedback?"

Project: Personal Branding and Content Creation

Phase 1: Introduction to AI and Prompt Engineering

Students will learn the basics of artificial intelligence, machine learning, and how large language models function. They will be introduced to prompt engineering and learn how to communicate effectively with AI systems for simple tasks.

Key Topics:

- Overview of AI, machine learning, and LLMs
- Basic prompt engineering (all the components of the RICE framework)

Phase 2: Advanced Prompt Techniques (simultaneous with phases 3-5)

Building on foundational skills, students will explore advanced techniques in crafting prompts to elicit precise and useful outputs from AI systems. These advanced techniques will be introduced to students as they encounter challenges for which these techniques can offer solutions.

Key Topics:

- Advanced prompt engineering (reiteration, chain-of-thought, delimiters, in-context, prompt chaining, AI-assisted prompting)
- Strategies for refining AI outputs

Phase 3: Personal Brand Development

The teacher will lead brainstorming sessions on what makes a personal brand effective. Students will explore their personal strengths and interests to develop a unique brand identity, using AI to assist in brainstorming and creativity.

Key Topics:

- Using AI to reflect on personal strengths
- Crafting a brand story
- Generative AI logo design

Sample Prompts:

- "Act as a personal branding expert. Ask me one question at a time to learn more about me so you can help me to create my personal brand. Tell me when you have enough information about me and then suggest 3-5 ideas for me to consider."
- "Create a short brand story based on these experiences: [list experiences]."
- "Brainstorm and describe ideas for a logo that reflects my interests in [topic]."

Phase 4: Content Creation and Curation

Students will create various types of content, utilizing AI tools to enhance and refine their work, focusing on quality and creativity.

Key Topics:

- AI-assisted content creation (videos, newsletters, social media posts)
- Structuring and editing content for impact

Sample Prompts:

- "Suggest a structure for a newsletter about [topic]."
- "What are some engaging video content ideas for [audience]? Explain your reasoning."
- "How can I visually enhance the following social media post so as to maximize viewer engagement?"

Phase 5: Content Planning and Strategy

Students will develop a strategic approach to content creation, including planning, goal setting, and understanding audience needs. The teacher will work with students to ensure that they can hold themselves accountable for their goals and tasks.

Key Topics:

- Using AI to manage a content calendar
- Setting goals and objectives
- Analyzing audience needs with AI

Sample Prompts:

- "Help me create a content calendar for the next month. The goal is maximum impact for each post/newsletter/video. Your first task is to describe different systems, routines, and habits for me to consider so that I can be consistent and effective."
- "As an expert in marketing, which goals and objectives are worth focusing on, and which ones might appear obvious but aren't actually as useful?"
- "Analyze the described audience and suggest content topics. Audience: [description] "

Phase 6: Presentation and Reflection

Students will present their personal brand and content portfolio, reflecting on their learning journey and personal growth.

Key Topics:

- Effective presentation skills
- Reflective writing on content creation
- Evaluating personal growth and understanding

Teacher Support with AI

Teachers can use AI to learn more about the topics of this course and guide students in developing their personal brands and content creation skills.

Sample Prompts:

- "I have to teach a class on personal branding and content creation, and I know nothing about these two topics. Explain the most basic principles to me in simple language."
- "What should I look for in a student's sample social media post to evaluate its effectiveness?"
- "Generate a Do/Don't list to guide students in developing their personal brands."

These two ideas—creating and developing a business plan, and personal branding and content creation—are both centered on achieving real-world results that stem from students' unique interests, creativity, and ingenuity. AI is leveraged by both the students and the teacher to learn more about the topics and concepts that pertain to these projects. As a result, students learn real-world and interdisciplinary skills that can apply to various future endeavors, including how to leverage AI to learn and create. These are not the only project ideas that will accomplish this, but any effective project and learning plan for a class on AI and prompt engineering will have similar characteristics.

It's worth noting that these projects may necessitate other kinds of generated content, like images. Remember that fluency with LLMs is transferable. All someone needs to know to apply the same skill to image generation is the proper vocabulary. The extent to which this is feasible for schools depends on the AI tools available. I expect the list of such tools to grow with time.

Through these projects, students will discover that high-quality work requires human creativity and ingenuity in the driver's seat. This is why it's important for students to undertake projects of personal importance to them, and why the quality of the final product should be their guiding motivation.

You can outsource a task to AI, but not a vision.

If students want to try making their lives easier by having AI do the work for them, I say let them try. If they are truly dedicated to a vision and focused on the quality of the work, then they'll quickly discover that they'll never be satisfied with AI output accepted at face value. They'll need to provide feedback, rewrite prompts, and edit AI's work—and at the end of it all, they'll discover that the results that they need will require hard work. And there will still be plenty of times when they realize they're better off doing something themselves.

In the end, it's not just about instructing AI to execute a task—it's about knowing how to enlist the partnership of AI and produce high-quality work. Students will learn this best by leveraging AI in the pursuit of complex, real-world tasks that are born from their unique and creative visions. And in the process, they'll develop the proper mindset for an effective human-AI partnership and fill their toolbelts with all the necessary prompt engineering strategies, no matter the particular AI tool.

The result will be fluency in AI, preparing students for a future where AI collaboration is increasingly prevalent and essential.

CHAPTER
06

SEVEN STEPS FOR INTEGRATING AI INTO EDUCATION

We first needed to know what artificial intelligence is and isn't before we could learn how generative AI systems like large language models work. We needed to know how LLMs work so that we could then learn prompt engineering and take full advantage of this technology to accomplish complex tasks. We needed to become prompt engineers so we could understand what it takes to teach students to become fluent in AI.

Now that we've done all that, it's time to zoom out and explore how AI fits into the broader K-12 education landscape. This includes introducing students to AI and teaching them how to use it across the curriculum and without the kind of dedicated course or unit described in the previous chapter. We'll also dive into several other issues, like professional development and community transparency.

Consider this your playbook for integrating AI in education.

First, recognize that AI requires a different approach

Artificial intelligence is not educational technology—it's a general-purpose technology with significant ramifications for education.

A general-purpose technology (the original GPT) is one that has broad applications for society and can trigger significant transformations across multiple industries and sectors. Examples include the internet, telephones, and electricity. These technologies have reshaped how we live, work, and interact with the world around us.

Contrast this with the likes of smartboards and Google Classroom. These are technologies created specifically for education. They offer real benefits and have improved the educational experience, but they haven't had revolutionary impacts on society. AI, on the other hand, was not created for the classroom, and is a game-changing technology with significant real-world impacts across many domains. It's crucial to understand that AI is not education technology—it's technology that impacts education.

AI is changing the ways people work, create, learn, and play, and its impact is being felt far more quickly in professional spaces than in educational ones. On any random day you're likely to find stories in the news about the impact of AI on a given company or industry. And the innovation fueled by this technology is moving far faster among individuals than among institutions, leaving us with immeasurable new approaches for many of life's tasks both big and small.

As such, educators need to treat this technology differently than previous new technologies we've brought into the classroom. We can't spend a day of professional development learning about AI, ask ourselves "how can we use this?" and then expect to derive benefits. That approach might work for other tools or applications, but not AI.

AI needs to be studied in its own natural habitat. What does that mean? It means the real world, outside of education, across industries and professions. The work that people do across the professional world is being impacted by AI, and we can't thoroughly make sense of AI in education without understanding what's happening "out there."

Go to an AI-powered search engine like Copilot or Perplexity and ask it to summarize the latest news in artificial intelligence. You can see these AI-fueled changes unfolding in real time. Understanding these real-world applications is crucial for educators because it provides context for understanding AI as well as the skills and knowledge students will need for their future careers.

Yes, there's a disclaimer here: much of today's AI hype won't survive in the coming years, even though we can clearly see some of its impact now. Nevertheless, we can look past the bursting of the hype bubble and confidently say that AI will be a force to be reckoned with in the future. The best approach is to be skeptical in the short term, optimistic in the long term—and prepare students for that long-term future.

In the short term, we should question bold claims about AI's capabilities by experiencing those capabilities for ourselves, critically evaluate AI tools that are advertised to schools, and stay informed about the latest developments in AI and its impact on the world.

In the long term, we should be open to the transformative potential of AI, plan for a world where AI is a common tool across various professions, and teach students how to enlist AI's assistance to accomplish complex tasks. By adopting this balanced approach, we can develop a realistic understanding of AI's current limitations while also preparing students for future possibilities.

But this approach requires a thorough understanding of how AI works and a recognition that it requires a completely different strategy than we're used to.

Second, learn by doing

Once we recognize that AI requires a different approach, how do we begin? To understand the roles AI could or should play in education, learn how to use it hands-on.

The use cases, possibilities, and limitations for AI in education will be far easier to identify after stakeholders learn how AI works through practical experience. With AI, you can't just learn about it—you have to learn by "doing" it.

This is why professional development, both for teachers and administrators, needs to focus on learning prompt engineering and using AI before entertaining any discussions of policy, ethics, and appropriate use. These discussions are still important, but they become much more meaningful and fruitful when grounded in practical experience.

In line with the general-purpose technology ethos, professional development with AI shouldn't start with education-related tasks. Instead, begin with tasks that everyone faces in their daily lives. My favorite task to use is cooking. LLM chatbots can do wonders for meal planning, recipes, and cooking tips that can be customized to each family's unique needs—and every family needs to eat. Take the strategies discussed in Chapter 4 and try them for yourself.

This approach to introducing AI will help to overcome hesitance towards the new technology, which is a common occurrence in education. Once educators see how AI works and what it can do in familiar contexts, they'll naturally start to experiment with its use cases in the classroom, such as lesson planning.

This hands-on approach is crucial because innovation is a ground-up phenomenon. Individuals doing the daily work understand their needs best. When they discover a solution that will make things easier, more efficient, or of higher quality, they won't hesitate to take advantage.

But this is the opposite of how a lot of professional development works. Showing teachers with limited AI backgrounds how they can use an LLM to write a lesson plan is counterproductive. Instead, when teachers understand how AI works through practical experience, they'll find the proper use cases for their needs.

Consider a history teacher who discovers how AI can help create unique meal plans to accommodate a child recently diagnosed with celiac disease. With a newfound appreciation for what AI can do, they then experiment with it to generate multiple-choice questions for a quiz. After that, they realize its potential for creating personalized study guides for students struggling with specific topics.

And teachers talk. As they experiment and discover new approaches to common struggles, word will spread. That history teacher will share that innovation for creating personalized study guides in their next department meeting.

The best thing education leaders can do is to facilitate the sharing of what works and doesn't work, as learned by trial and error. This could involve:

- Setting up forums for teachers to share their AI experiences
- Organizing regular "AI in education" roundtable discussions
- Creating an e-mail newsletter showcasing successful AI applications in various subjects and grade levels

The path to effectively integrating AI in education isn't through top-down directives or theoretical discussions. It's through hands-on experience, experimentation, and collaborative learning. By allowing educators to explore AI's capabilities in both everyday and educational contexts, they will unlock its true potential in the classroom.

Remember: to understand how AI can transform education, you first need to experience how it can transform everyday tasks.

Third, ask questions (but don't rush the answers)

As stakeholders develop an understanding of how AI works, what it can and can't do, and observe its impact on the world, many questions about AI in education will become clearer. Issues pertaining to cheating, critical thinking, and personalized tutoring are easier to discuss after developing fluency in AI. However, just because they're easier to discuss doesn't mean they're easier to answer.

The fundamental purpose of education is to prepare students for the world they will inhabit as adults. But what happens when that world is changing at an unprecedented pace?

AI is reshaping the very fabric of society, work, and human interaction. As a result, education finds itself at a crossroads, forced to question and potentially overhaul practices that have been standard for generations.

This situation demands that we grapple with uncomfortable questions that challenge the core of what we believe about education. For example:

- Is the essay obsolete when AI can write them for us? Or are the human ideas, prompt writing, and iteration with AI the new skills to learn, instead of traditional writing?

- Should we embrace personalized AI tutoring to help disadvantaged students, or do we risk leading to the replacement of some human teachers?

- When prompt engineering requires precise and accurate word choice, do we need to shift more focus in curricula to essential content-specific vocabulary?

- Do we need to revisit the guidance we offer students pertaining to their career choices? Should we be aware of which jobs are at greater risk of automation or might see a decrease in demand for human labor?

These questions challenge how we think about assessing critical thinking and communication, how we balance leveraging technology for equity while maintaining the human element in teaching, our approach to knowledge perceived as lower-order or higher-order, and what it means to be "college and career ready."

They are uncomfortable questions because they force us to confront the possibility that many of our long-standing educational practices may no longer be relevant or effective in an AI-driven world. They challenge us to reconsider what skills are truly essential for future success and how best to cultivate them. Sometimes we may conclude that new skills, like prompt engineering, are essential. Other times we may conclude that we need to double down on the "old-school" ways.

The discomfort these questions provoke is not just intellectual; it's also emotional and professional. For many of us, these questions challenge our identity and the value of our life's work. It's natural to feel defensive or resistant when faced with such fundamental challenges to established norms.

However, it's crucial to remember that education has always evolved to meet the changing needs of society. Just as the industrial revolution transformed education in the 19th and 20th centuries, the AI revolution is poised to do the same in the 21st century. Our task is not to resist this change, but to shape it in a way that best serves our students and society.

These are the conversations schools need to have before trying to draw the line between when it's "cheating" and "not cheating" to use AI. After all, how can you call something "cheating" when it's becoming the norm in the professional world? But answering questions like these will not come quickly nor easily, and the answers will differ from one community to the next. They will require serious contemplation and debate, with input from all stakeholder groups in a deliberate and purposeful fashion.

It's tempting to jump to a policy. Every school system has an incentive to appear at the vanguard of each innovation. It's reassuring for community members to know that their schools are on top of integrating emerging technologies. But the desire to answer questions quickly may lead to the wrong answers. Consider the current national discourse on issues pertaining to cell phones and social media. We let the genie out of the bottle before we fully understood its influence.

With technology like AI, prioritize long-term and sustainable effectiveness. The short term may be messy, but it will be worth it.

Take your time. Convene a study group (maybe multiple groups) of teachers, administrators, parents, and even students to share news stories about the impacts of AI on the world, reflect on experiences about using AI for tasks in every-one's personal lives, and share best practices for prompt engineering. Engage in open, honest discussions about the challenges and opportunities AI presents. Encourage stakeholders to voice their concerns and ideas, fostering an environment of collaborative problem-solving.

The important conversations won't be any less uncomfortable, but they'll be a lot easier to have when grounded in the practical experiences of studying and using AI. By taking our time to grapple with these uncomfortable questions, we can help ensure that education remains relevant, effective, and truly preparatory for the AI-augmented future our students will face.

Fourth, prioritize being good at your "job"

As stakeholders become fluent in AI and observe its impact on the world, they'll come to learn one of the most crucial lessons: the ability to evaluate AI output is the linchpin of successful integration. This evaluation skill is what separates effective AI use from potentially dangerous misapplication.

In the professional world, the primary deterrent to misusing AI isn't a set of rules, but rather the risk of real-world consequences if one gets it wrong. What prevents your lawyer, accountant, or doctor from using AI for their job is the consequence of what happens if they rely on poor AI-generated content and therefore produce poor results. The risks of losing a client, being fired, or endangering a patient's health are too grave for them to rely on AI output they can't trust. But if these individuals can confidently utilize AI-generated content, they will undoubtedly leverage AI to enhance their efficiency and the quality of their work.

Ergo, the important skill for students to learn is how to evaluate AI-generated output for its usefulness.[3]

If you fail to recognize when AI has provided unreliable information and incorporate it into a significant project, the result will be compromised. Conversely, if you lack the discernment to recognize when AI offers an innovative, out-of-the-box solution, you risk overlooking valuable ideas. This is the difference between being replaced by someone who knows how to use AI and being the replacer.

The secret to evaluating AI output? Content expertise.

Let's revisit your lawyer, accountant, and doctor. The lawyer with extensive legal knowledge will have the intuition to detect when AI-generated content might contain inaccurate information, prompting them to verify and cross-check. The experienced accountant can discern when an AI-suggested tax strategy is creative while staying within legal boundaries. And a skilled doctor can recognize when an AI-assisted diagnosis aligns with observed symptoms and medical history, or when it requires further investigation.

These professionals' confidence in using AI stems from their content-specific expertise, which allows them to critically evaluate AI output. This expertise enables them to successfully delegate routine tasks, deepen their understanding of complex topics, and uncover novel ideas worth pursuing. The result is more successful case outcomes, more creative financial strategies, and more accurate medical diagnoses. (Plus, they get to charge a lot more for their superior work.)

AI makes you better at your job when you're already good at your job. So becoming good at your job is the first step to using AI successfully.

---

3   I use the term *usefulness* purposely, rather than a term like accuracy. That's because usefulness is more encompassing. AI-generated output isn't useful if it's inaccurate. But it's also not useful if it is accurate but not relevant to the overarching goal.

If we apply the same principle to the classroom, then students must first become knowledgeable enough to evaluate the usefulness of AI-generated output. When they're good at their "job" (i.e., the subject matter), they'll be prepared to enlist AI to become *even better* at it.

Fifth, identify expertise benchmarks

This leads to the next question: At what point in a content area curriculum can students demonstrate sufficient expertise to effectively evaluate AI output and begin using AI?

Let's call these points "expertise benchmarks." Administrators and teachers need to determine appropriate expertise benchmarks in each subject area, based on student-demonstrated content mastery, to guide when AI can be introduced. These benchmarks should be specific and reflect the core competencies required in each discipline.

For example, in a high school English class, an expertise benchmark might be the ability to analyze literary devices in complex texts. Once students consistently demonstrate this skill, they might be ready to use AI to generate initial analyses, which they would then critically evaluate and expand upon. In a middle school science course, an expertise benchmark could be understanding the scientific method and basic experimental design. After reaching this benchmark, students might use AI to brainstorm hypotheses or experimental setups, which they would then refine based on their scientific knowledge.

The important ingredient in these and any situation in which AI is introduced is what happens next. Students need to see AI-generated content and ask, "Is this a good response? Do I understand it? Is this information useful to me? Does it require fact-checking, validation, or editing?" Answering these questions and appropriately evaluating AI-generated content relies on subject matter knowledge. This is the key that underlies all potential expertise benchmarks.

Any given subject, grade, or class could have one or more expertise benchmarks. The idea is to identify a baseline of content knowledge needed before introducing AI. Every time we evaluate an AI-generated response, we do so through the context of knowledge we already have. Therefore, it's important to first define what kind of knowledge is necessary to take advantage of such a resource.

In sum: before you introduce AI to a student of any age or in any subject matter, you first need to be confident that they can independently evaluate the usefulness of AI-generated responses.

Sixth, create a structured and versatile framework

Once these expertise benchmarks are defined, AI can be introduced through a combination of traditional instruction on prompt engineering and a traffic light system:

- **Red light** = "Don't use AI for this task."
- **Yellow light** = "You may or may not be able to use AI, as determined on a case-by-case basis at teacher discretion."
- **Green light** = "You have full liberty to use AI as much as you want, but know that you're accountable for the quality and accuracy of the final product."

Red light activities focus on developing foundational content knowledge and interdisciplinary critical thinking skills. While AI might be used as an example (such as having students evaluate AI-produced content), the primary goal is to prepare students to use AI independently, which first requires being competent without it.

Yellow light activities can vary widely. They might involve: the initial stages of a project, like brainstorming; personalized tutoring, like asking AI to explain concepts in simpler terms; or quality improvement, like editing student writing. In these situations, students prompt and evaluate AI under teacher supervision. Teachers must leverage their pedagogical expertise to guide students and should expect to say things like: "You can't use AI for that right now, but you can use it to do this instead. Here are some ways to prompt it. Show me what it produces, and we'll discuss the next steps." Yellow light activities also rely on the teacher's understanding of AI and prompt engineering, which is why the professional development approach discussed earlier is so important.

Green light activities simulate real-world scenarios: the final product is what matters, and students are responsible for its quality and accuracy, regardless of AI use. These activities simulate the risk-reward calculus associated with AI use that professionals face. Students need to decide whether and how to use AI—based on their judgment of if and how it can help them to achieve better results—just as professionals do. The only difference is that the stakes are a lot lower in the classroom (where you might earn a bad grade) than in the workplace (where you might be fired).

Green light activities develop the crucial mindset of being the human in charge, leading the human-AI partnership, and making informed decisions about AI-generated output. This approach prepares students for a future where AI is likely to be a common professional tool and in which independent, accurate, and high-quality work is expected of them.

On the whole, identifying expertise benchmarks and then gradually introducing AI to students through a traffic light system will balance competing goals. It will help to ensure that students:

- First, develop the content expertise and thinking skills needed to evaluate AI-generated output.

- Second, are guided through strategies for communicating with AI to elicit useful output.

- Third, can independently decide when and how to leverage the human-AI partnership to increase performance while holding themselves accountable for accuracy and quality.

By implementing this comprehensive approach to AI integration in education, we can prepare students not only to use AI effectively but also to engage with it responsibly and critically in their future academic and professional lives. This system acknowledges the transformative potential of AI while emphasizing the enduring importance of human expertise and critical thinking.

In essence, it fosters fluency in AI.

Seventh, engage in transparent communication

It's important to note the disparity between the AI that students have access to at school and the AI they have access to at home.

While schools are constrained in regard to AI, students often have unfettered access to a wide array of AI tools outside the classroom. At the time of writing, Google's Gemini and Microsoft's Copilot are integrated with those companies' search engines and apps, Meta AI is integrated with multiple social media platforms, and ChatGPT, Claude, and Perplexity can be accessed for free through their websites and apps (and these are not the only AI tools out there). These platforms are available for students at home, but not in school.

The reasons for this disparity are multifaceted. Schools must navigate a complex web of data privacy laws, which often slows the adoption of new technologies. Additionally, the implementation of AI in educational settings requires significant financial investments and the appropriate technology infrastructure. Conversely, AI access at home primarily depends on parental permission and supervision, which can vary widely from household to household.

Simply put, schools are not equipped to keep up with the real world.

This situation creates challenges. Students with unrestricted access to AI at home may be tempted to use these tools for homework or assignments in ways that compromise learning objectives. This could lead to everything from confusion about when and how to use these tools to a disparity in skills—both in terms of using AI and building the foundational knowledge needed to be more effective with AI.

To address these challenges, schools must prioritize transparency and communication with families about their AI strategies. This approach should include:

1. Involving parents in AI study groups (where everyone learns to use AI) and policy discussions to ensure diverse perspectives are considered.

2. Transparent communication regarding expertise benchmarks, prompt engineering instruction, and the traffic light system for including AI in learning activities, and regular updates about those plans—including timelines and rationales.

3. Offering informational sessions for parents to learn about AI, its impact on the world, and the ramifications for education.

4. Encouraging ongoing conversations between teachers, parents, and students about AI experiences—both positive and negative.

5. Developing and communicating clear guidelines for when and how to use AI at home.

Let's double-click on those guidelines.

Guidelines for AI use are most effective when written after a thorough framework for AI instruction is established (see above: expertise benchmarks and a traffic light system). This will ensure clarity and consistency, and minimize confusion.

It's understandable that schools, in an attempt to address the rapidly evolving impact of AI on education, might seek to quickly issue guidelines for AI use before establishing a comprehensive instructional framework. However, without that framework and broader context (once again: grounded in practical hands-on experience with AI), such hastily crafted guidelines can potentially do more harm than good. This approach, while well-intentioned, often falls short of addressing the complex realities of AI in education and can lead to confusion, inconsistency, and ineffective implementation.

For AI guidelines to be truly effective, they must be shared in the context of a comprehensive instructional framework that is born of real-world study, hands-on experience, and curriculum-focused decisions. Once this is done, guidelines can then be written to inform the community of:

1. **Clear Timeline for AI Integration**: Families need to know when and why students can expect to start using AI tools in their educational journey. This timeline should be grade-specific, subject-specific, and aligned to expertise benchmarks.

2. **Specific AI Tools and Platforms**: Schools should clearly communicate which AI tools and platforms will be used in the classroom. This information helps parents understand and potentially explore these tools at home, fostering a cohesive learning environment.

3. **Detailed Usage Scenarios**: Guidelines should include specific examples of how AI might be used in different subjects and for various types of assignments. This could include scenarios for brainstorming, research assistance, writing support, or problem-solving.

4. **Assessment Policies**: Clearly communicating how AI use will be factored into assessments and grading is crucial. This includes a detailed explanation of the traffic light system.

While it's unfeasible to prevent students from accessing AI outside of school, a united approach among parents, teachers, and administrators can help guide students towards using (or refraining from using) AI in ways that support the pedagogical goals of content expertise and interdisciplinary critical thinking skills. By aligning home and school messaging about AI, we can better support the ultimate goal of AI fluency.

CONCLUSION:
THE SURPRISING WAY TO RULE THE AI-INFUSED WORLD

Dear Reader,

I hope you've learned a lot from this book.

I hope you now have a better understanding of what artificial intelligence is, why it matters, and how to use it. I hope you've been fruitful in experimenting with prompt engineering strategies to accomplish a variety of tasks. And I hope that you have a clearer idea of how to approach AI in education and how to teach students to become fluent in AI.

But alas, that's not enough. There's one more point I want to make before you put this book down. It doesn't *quite* fit in with understanding and teaching prompt engineering and AI, but it's one of the most important ideas on the topic. So I decided to make it the conclusion, as I think it's a fitting capstone on this technology-heavy deep dive.

But first, I want to reiterate my aspirational hopes: to contribute to the conversation. If you walk away from this with new and interesting ideas to think and talk about, then I consider my mission to be accomplished.

Thank you,

Aaron

The future does not belong to the technologist

Generative AI democratizes content creation.

Thanks to these tools, anyone can easily create, share, and sell text, image, audio, and video content (evidenced by yours truly). This democratization, while empowering, presents a new challenge: the world is now flooded with content of varying quality. And since the ultimate arbiter of quality is consumer judgment in the jungles of the market, there's nothing stopping the world from being flooded with low-quality content that consumers then must sift through.

Sorting through the haystack to find the needle is one thing, but what's even more challenging is creating the needle and making sure it gets found.

If AI is a means to an end, then the end is creating high-quality content that thrives. This isn't just a matter of books that sell or social media posts that go viral. It's also a matter of presentations given to clients, reports written for senior analysts, research articles to be published, and any other content created for personal or professional purposes. All this content can be created by or enhanced with generative AI, making the market that much more competitive—not just for content, but for ideas.

Being fluent in AI helps, and it helps a lot (obviously). Students who develop the instincts for partnering with AI, effectively communicating with it, and critically evaluating its output will be able to produce work of superior quality. However, creating standout content and ensuring its visibility requires something deeper than just technical proficiency.

When we are inundated with content, we are awash in answers. When answers become cheap and abundant, the right question becomes invaluable. Allow me to say it again:

A world flooded with content is a world flooded with answers—and when answers become cheap and abundant, the right question becomes invaluable.

Standing out in this content-rich environment begins with asking different questions. These questions, in turn, stem from a deeper understanding—not just of technology, but of everything that shapes our world.

When we comprehend a problem more fully, we naturally ask better questions. And we better understand a problem when we more fully understand the *experiences* of those facing the problem.

And that's the core of it: understanding the human experience.

Being able to see the world through someone else's eyes, to articulate opposing points of view, and to understand the grand forces that wrought this moment in time—these abilities are the sparks that light the fires of great questions.

Let's revisit our marketing professional tasked with creating an ad campaign for a new product. An AI-fluent marketer might use generative AI to quickly produce multiple ad copy variants or generate visual concepts. However, a marketer with a deep human understanding might instinctively recognize the target audience's unspoken needs, like how they're looking for a product they can use and be confident that they're not inadvertently contributing to environmental damage. That understanding will have important ramifications for the final ad campaign.

It's not just a matter of using technology to do a job better and more efficiently. Rather, it's a matter of understanding how the job meets the needs of people seeking a solution (and then using technology to do that job better and more efficiently). And understanding the needs of people has nothing to do with technology.

This leads us to a paradox. Education needs to prepare students for an increasingly technology-centric world; but to thrive in that world, students need to see people and problems without technology getting in the way.

How do we square that circle? By doubling down on the time-honored basics that have endured for centuries: the arts and humanities.

Music, art, literature, and history show us what it means to be human. These subjects don't just teach us—they allow us to *experience* diverse perspectives, places, and times different from our own. They remind us that everyone is connected through a web of actions, all influenced by how well we do or don't understand each other.

There's a reason why business, political, and military leaders often turn to history and philosophy. Ancient wisdom, born from making sense of the human experience, remains as relevant today as it was millennia ago. And anyone whose world hasn't been frozen by that piece of music, enraptured staring at that painting, or brought to tears by that performance is no more human than their AI sidekick.

And as a music teacher, let me tell you: if you think your favorite music is life-changing, imagine being the one on stage making it happen, building indescribable relationships with fellow musicians, artists, performers, and most importantly the audience.

Participating in music and the arts, reading literature, discussing history and philosophy—these are the things that teach us what it means to be, feel, and understand our collective humanity.

When students develop a deep, authentic understanding of the human experience, they gain the most valuable lens through which to view real-world challenges. They'll be able to empathize with a client, patient, or peer. They'll be able to articulate the opposing desires of a negotiating partner. They'll be able to analyze a social or workplace dynamic and realize which gears of the system need to be greased.

This combination of empathy, articulation, and experiential understanding, when paired with domain expertise, enables students to ask the most pertinent and insightful questions.

While fluency in AI is undoubtedly an important skill in the modern world, it's merely a means to an end. AI can assist in producing high-quality work, but it cannot determine what work is important to produce. This discernment remains a uniquely human capability.

Only those individuals who have developed a deep under-standing of the world around them will know which questions to ask, which tasks to prioritize, and how to identify which solu-tions are most appropriate and impactful.

Leveraging technology to accomplish complex tasks is the skill of the future, but the future itself belongs to the fine arts and humanities.

To cultivate this level of human understanding, we need to embrace "unplugged" education in these subjects alongside study of emerging technologies like artificial intelligence.

Unplugged education is about creating intentional spaces and experiences free from digital distractions, where students can engage deeply with ideas and with each other. These ex-periences might include face-to-face discussions, hands-on tactile experiences in art and nature, community engagement, or reading a good old-fashioned physical book in a quiet place where thoughts can flourish.

These unplugged experiences don't just complement digital learning—they're the prerequisites for a digital world, helping students develop a more rounded set of skills and perspec-tives essential for navigating an AI-infused future.

With such experiences, students will develop a richer understanding of the human condition. This understanding becomes the foundation for asking better questions, producing more innovative solutions, and ultimately building a better world.

The future belongs not just to those who can work with AI, but to those who can leverage AI to address the most fundamental human needs and aspirations. By balancing AI fluency with a deep understanding of the human experience, we can prepare students to not just survive, but thrive in the world of tomorrow.

Made in the USA
Columbia, SC
01 November 2024